THE PRESIDENT'S ALMANAC

BY PAULA N. KESSLER AND JUSTIN SEGAL

ILLUSTRATIONS BY JUSTIN SEGAL

Lowell 🏠 House
Juvenile
Los Angeles

CONTEMPORARY BOOKS
Chicago

for Aaron, who can be whatever he wants to be. P.N.K.
to Margie, for sharing in my love of history. J.S.

PHOTO CREDITS:
cover: National Archives, George Washington; The White House, Bill Clinton
insides: National Archives: pp. 8, 9, 10, 12, 13, 14, 16, 18, 19, 20, 21, 22, 23, 24, 25, 27, 28, 29, 30, 31, 32, 33, 35, 36, 37, 38, 39, 40, 41, 42, 43, 44, 45, 46, 47; Bush Presidential Materials Project: pp. 49, 50, 51, 52; courtesy of The White House: p. 53; courtesy of The Ohio Historical Society: p. 28

Publisher: Jack Artenstein
Vice President, Juvenile Division: Elizabeth Amos
Director of Publishing Services: Rena Copperman
Managing Editor, Juvenile Division: Lindsey Hay
Editor in Chief, Juvenile Nonfiction: Amy Downing
Art Director: Lisa-Theresa Lenthall
Designer and Typesetter: Justin Segal
Cover Design: Justin Segal

Library of Congress Catalog Card Number: 96-390

ISBN: 1-56565-379-3

Lowell House books can be purchased at special discounts when ordered in bulk for premiums and special sales. Contact Department JH at the following address:

Lowell House Juvenile
2029 Century Park East, Suite 3290
Los Angeles, CA 90067

Manufactured in the United States of America
10 9 8 7 6 5 4 3 2

Contents

PREAMBLE _____ 4

WHAT IS A PRESIDENT? _____ 5

MEET THE PRESIDENTS _____ 8

CHILDHOOD STORIES _____ 54

EARLY ADVENTURES _____ 57

THE CAMPAIGN TRAIL _____ 63

TAKING THE OATH _____ 68

PRESIDENTIAL DAYS _____ 71

FIRST LADIES _____ 80

FAMILY LIFE _____ 84

LATER YEARS _____ 91

LEGENDS LEFT BEHIND _____ 94

INDEX _____ 96

Preamble

Get ready for a wonderful journey!

In *The Presidents Almanac* you will find amazing stories and fun facts about some of the most important people in the world . . . the presidents of the United States.

You'll learn who can be president and what a president does. You'll see what makes each of our presidents unique. You'll read about presidential families, and even what presidents did for fun when they were growing up.

From George Washington to Bill Clinton, this book is an exciting journey through more than two hundred years of American history . . . and a journey we have enjoyed very much.

We hope you will enjoy it, too.

Paula N. Kessler and Justin Segal

What Is a President?

Every four years, the American people elect a person to one of the most important jobs in the world, president of the United States. But just what *is* a president?

In 1776, when America's thirteen colonies declared themselves a new nation, they needed a leader to help strengthen the cause of freedom and independence. Up until that time, many leaders of other countries were kings and queens who had inherited their power or had taken control of their country by force. America, which had been ruled by the King of England, King George III, was a new nation with different ideas. Americans needed their own system of government . . . and a different kind of leader. The thirteen colonies even wanted a new title for that leader and chose the Latin word *praesidens*, which means "to preside" or "to rule."

In 1787, the people chose representatives to act as "delegates" at a Constitutional Convention. At this meeting, it was decided that America's new leader would be chosen according to the will of the people, and would govern by a written code called The Constitution, which we still live by today.

HOW IS OUR PRESIDENT DIFFERENT FROM OTHER LEADERS?

There are many ways in which America's president is different from other world leaders:

He is elected to office every four years, with a maximum of two terms (eight years) in office. Some countries allow presidents to be elected over and over again, or limit them to a single term.

- The title and duties of president cannot be inherited, even though America's presidents have sometimes been related. In cases where the president is no longer able to carry out his (or, hopefully, someday her) elective duties, the role of president passes to the vice-president.

- A president is bound by the same laws as every other American. If he breaks the law, he can be fined, arrested, or removed from office.

THREE BRANCHES OF AMERICAN GOVERNMENT

America's system of government has three branches:

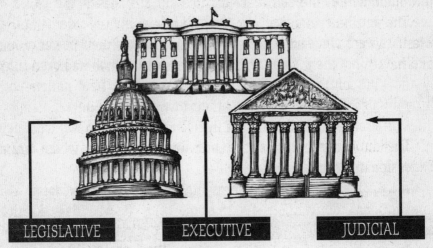

| LEGISLATIVE | EXECUTIVE | JUDICIAL |

The President leads the executive branch, which includes many agencies and the president's Cabinet departments.

The legislative branch contains the two houses of Congress—the House of Representatives and the Senate. The House of Representatives has 435 elected members representing each state in the nation according to their population, with at least one representative from each state. They are elected every two years. The Senate has 100 members, consisting of two representatives from each state, who are elected to serve a six-year term.

The judicial branch is headed by the Supreme Court, which oversees the federal judicial system and decides issues of Constitutional law.

Because these three branches of government are separate, they help keep too much power from being given to any one person, including the president himself.

WHO CAN BE PRESIDENT?

Americans have always been proud to say that "anyone can grow up to become president." Our presidents have come in all shapes and sizes. They have all had different lives and experiences. Many have been lawyers or military leaders before being elected to the White House. Others have been teachers, shopkeepers, farmers . . . even movie stars. After leaving office, some of America's presidents have been forgotten, while others are remembered all over the world.

The rules for being able to run for president are very simple. A president must be born a U.S. citizen, be at least thirty-five years old, and have lived in the United States for at least fourteen years. That's it!

THE DUTIES OF THE PRESIDENT

The duties and powers of a president, according to the United States Constitution, are as follows:

1. The president is Commander-in-Chief of the armed forces.
2. He meets with the leaders of foreign countries.
3. He has the power to make treaties with other countries.
4. He has the power to appoint ambassadors and judges.
5. He must make certain America's laws are upheld.
6. He has the power to grant pardons and reprieves to criminals.
7. He is required to report to Congress on "the State of the Union," although he is not required to report on any particular subject or at any particular time during the year.

Now that you know a little bit about what a president does and who can be president, read on to discover the inside scoop on the men who have led the United States!

Meet the Presidents

George Washington

Born into a poor family, George Washington had little formal education, never went to college, and was orphaned at age fifteen. By age twenty-one, he decided to become a soldier and joined the Virginia militia, gradually working his way up to the rank of general.

General Washington survived many hardships while leading the colonists to victory in America's war for independence, called the Revolutionary War. Even though he was very shy and formal, he became so popular that there was talk of crowning him king. But Washington wanted to return to farming on his Virginia plantation. Still, he knew the new nation needed him. He was unanimously elected president by members of the Continental Congress, which represented each of the thirteen former colonies, now called the United States of America. Thus Washington became America's first president.

> **1ST PRESIDENT**
> FEDERALIST
> 1789–1797
> BORN: FEB 22. 1732
> DIED: DEC 14. 1799

> **WASHINGTON**
>
> "Everybody has a right to form and adopt whatever government they like best."
>
> **SPEAKS**

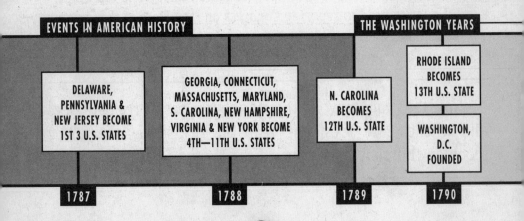

EVENTS IN AMERICAN HISTORY | THE WASHINGTON YEARS

DELAWARE, PENNSYLVANIA & NEW JERSEY BECOME 1ST 3 U.S. STATES

GEORGIA, CONNECTICUT, MASSACHUSETTS, MARYLAND, S. CAROLINA, NEW HAMPSHIRE, VIRGINIA & NEW YORK BECOME 4TH—11TH U.S. STATES

N. CAROLINA BECOMES 12TH U.S. STATE

RHODE ISLAND BECOMES 13TH U.S. STATE

WASHINGTON, D.C. FOUNDED

1787   1788   1789   1790

George Washington was the only president that didn't live in Washington, D.C. . . . it hadn't been created yet! He lived and was inaugurated in New York City. The Washington family moved to Philadelphia in 1790, when that city became the nation's temporary capital. When a site was finally chosen for America's government, it was named in honor of our first president.

John Adams

Patriotic Vocabulary

Federalist: One of the first political organizations in the United States, the **Federalist Party** believed in a strong national government and favored industry.

America owes much to its second president. John Adams was the man who insisted George Washington lead America's Revolutionary army. He also served as a key member of the Continental Congress and helped Thomas Jefferson write the Declaration of Independence. And it was Adams who traveled to Europe to borrow enough money to continue America's fight for freedom from England. It was no surprise that he earned the nickname "Atlas of Independence."

In 1798, he passed the Alien and Sedition Acts, laws which made it more difficult to become a U.S.

2ND PRESIDENT
FEDERALIST
1797–1801
BORN: OCT 30, 1735
DIED: JULY 4, 1826

THE ADAMS YEARS

| VERMONT BECOMES 14TH U.S. STATE | 1ST COLUMBUS DAY | U.S. NAVY ESTABLISHED | 1ST U.S. OPERA | 1ST PADDLE WHEEL STEAMBOAT |
| KENTUCKY BECOMES 15TH U.S. STATE | MEN'S POWDERED WIGS GO OUT OF FASHION | TENNESSEE BECOMES 16TH U.S. STATE | 1ST THERMOS BOTTLE |

| 1791 | 1792 | 1794 | 1796 | 1797 |

citizen and limited citizens' freedom to criticize the government.

Adams had a difficult time following the charismatic presidential example set by Washington. He was short and fat, with a sharp temper, nothing like the tall, stately Washington who was loved by all Americans.

Adams was the first president to live in the White House and the only president to be the father of another president, John Quincy Adams. He lived to be more than ninety, older than any other president, and died on the fiftieth anniversary of the Declaration of Independence.

Thomas Jefferson

Known as "Long John," Thomas Jefferson was 6 feet, 2 inches tall with a pink, freckled complexion and carrot-red hair.

Jefferson wrote the Declaration of Independence and was elected governor of Virginia in 1779 before he was elected president. He also served as secretary of state under Washington and as vice-president under Adams. Politics was his duty, but he had even greater passions: he was a scientist, musician, architect, and inventor. He was probably the most gifted president our nation has ever known.

3RD PRESIDENT
DEMOCRAT-
REPUBLICAN
1801–1809
BORN: APR 13, 1743
DIED: JULY 4, 1826

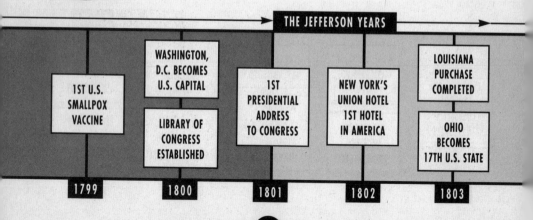

THE JEFFERSON YEARS

1ST U.S. SMALLPOX VACCINE	WASHINGTON, D.C. BECOMES U.S. CAPITAL		1ST PRESIDENTIAL ADDRESS TO CONGRESS	NEW YORK'S UNION HOTEL 1ST HOTEL IN AMERICA	LOUISIANA PURCHASE COMPLETED
	LIBRARY OF CONGRESS ESTABLISHED				OHIO BECOMES 17TH U.S. STATE
1799	1800		1801	1802	1803

JEFFERSON

"A little rebellion now and then is a good thing."

SPEAKS

Although Jefferson founded the U.S. Patent Office, he never applied for a patent on any of his own inventions, which included a revolving chair, a pedometer, a revolving music stand, and a letter-copying press.

He was our only president to design his own house, and he founded the University of Virginia, in Charlottesville.

Thomas Jefferson came from a large family, the third of ten children. He was a warm and playful man who liked to be with his wife, kids, and extended relatives. Thomas Jefferson's grandson, James Madison Randolph, was the first baby born in the White House.

James Madison

James Madison was a good-humored and modest man. He liked American fashions, and was the first president to wear modern trousers instead of knee-breeches.

While he was our smallest presi-

Patriotic Vocabulary

Secretary of State: There are fourteen executive departments in America's government, usually called the president's Cabinet. The **secretary of state** is the Cabinet member responsible for the government's foreign policy.

Democrat-Republican: The **Democrat-Republican Party** was organized by Thomas Jefferson and James Madison to oppose the Federalist Party. Its members believed in a weaker federal government, with more power given to the individual states. They also generally favored agriculture.

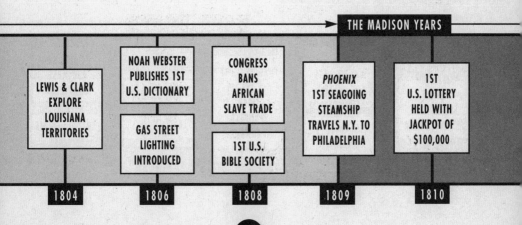

THE MADISON YEARS

LEWIS & CLARK EXPLORE LOUISIANA TERRITORIES

NOAH WEBSTER PUBLISHES 1ST U.S. DICTIONARY

GAS STREET LIGHTING INTRODUCED

CONGRESS BANS AFRICAN SLAVE TRADE

1ST U.S. BIBLE SOCIETY

PHOENIX 1ST SEAGOING STEAMSHIP TRAVELS N.Y. TO PHILADELPHIA

1ST U.S. LOTTERY HELD WITH JACKPOT OF $100,000

1804   1806   1808   1809   1810

dent at only 5 feet, 4 inches, Madison's size didn't affect his power. Before he was president, he spoke at the Constitutional Convention, a meeting to write and approve the U.S. Constitution. He stood so short that the other delegates could hardly see him, and he had a voice so weak they could barely hear him. Still, "the great little Madison" captured the attention of his fellow founding fathers. "If convincing is eloquence, James Madison was the most eloquent man I ever heard," a delegate said.

4TH PRESIDENT
DEMOCRAT-
REPUBLICAN
1809–1817
BORN: MAR 16, 1751
DIED: JUNE 28, 1836

During the War of 1812, when the British invaded Washington, D.C., Madison personally took command of the army.

After the war ended, Madison was forced to live in temporary housing while the executive mansion (which had been burned and damaged by the British army) was being repaired. White paint was used to cover the blackened fire marks, and ever since, the mansion became popularly known as the White House.

MADISON

"I flung forward the flag of the country."

SPEAKS

James Monroe

As a small boy, James Monroe walked several miles through the wilderness every day to go to school. He was considered an

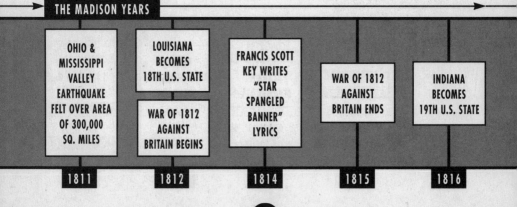

THE MADISON YEARS

OHIO & MISSISSIPPI VALLEY EARTHQUAKE FELT OVER AREA OF 300,000 SQ. MILES	LOUISIANA BECOMES 18TH U.S. STATE	FRANCIS SCOTT KEY WRITES "STAR SPANGLED BANNER" LYRICS	WAR OF 1812 AGAINST BRITAIN ENDS	INDIANA BECOMES 19TH U.S. STATE
	WAR OF 1812 AGAINST BRITAIN BEGINS			
1811	1812	1814	1815	1816

exceptional student, studying at Virginia's finest school, the Campbelltown Academy. In fact, he did so well with his studies (especially Latin and math), that he was able to enter college early, at age sixteen. A brilliant academic career seemed inevitable.

5TH PRESIDENT
DEMOCRAT-
REPUBLICAN
1817—1825
BORN: APR 28, 1758
DIED: JULY 4, 1831

The year was 1774, however, a time of great political upheaval in America as colonists began to break away from England and fight for their right to govern themselves. Monroe became caught up in the revolutionary spirit, even buying muskets (a type of gun) and marching with other students on the college grounds. By 1776, he quit his studies altogether, enlisting in Virginia's 3rd Infantry. Monroe returned to college in 1781, after the American Revolution had succeeded.

During his eight years in office, President Monroe was considered a calm and understanding leader. In 1823, President Monroe established the Monroe Doctrine, a document warning the countries of Europe not to create new colonies in the Americas. He worked very hard to help all Americans live together in harmony. His presidency was often called the "era of good feelings."

MONROE

"National honor is national property of the highest value."

SPEAKS

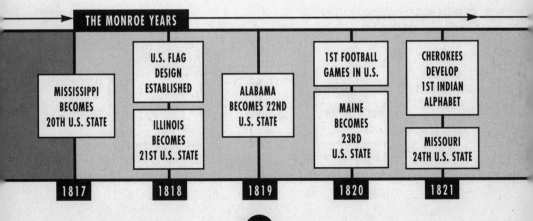

THE MONROE YEARS

| MISSISSIPPI BECOMES 20TH U.S. STATE | U.S. FLAG DESIGN ESTABLISHED | ILLINOIS BECOMES 21ST U.S. STATE | ALABAMA BECOMES 22ND U.S. STATE | 1ST FOOTBALL GAMES IN U.S. | MAINE BECOMES 23RD U.S. STATE | CHEROKEES DEVELOP 1ST INDIAN ALPHABET | MISSOURI 24TH U.S. STATE |

| 1817 | 1818 | 1819 | 1820 | 1821 |

John Quincy Adams

John Quincy Adams was born into politics and followed his father's footsteps. He wanted very much to be president, and even named one of his sons George Washington. In 1824, his wish was granted. Adams was elected by a single vote majority and became our nation's sixth chief executive.

6TH PRESIDENT
DEMOCRAT-
REPUBLICAN
1825—1829
BORN: JULY 11, 1767
DIED: FEB 23, 1848

As a boy, John Quincy Adams loved to spend time playing in the woods near the farm where he grew up in Braintree, Massachusetts. When he was just ten years old, he traveled to Europe with his father and learned to speak French fluently. It was in London, England that Adams met his future wife, Louisa Johnson. She became the only foreign-born first lady America ever had.

At 5 feet, 7 inches tall, with a plump body, and white sideburns on each side of his shiny bald head, John Quincy wasn't concerned with his appearance (he even wore the same hat for ten years!). Still, he was the first president to have his picture taken. He was also the first to publish a book of poetry and the first to serve in Congress (as a Massachusetts representative) after leaving the White House.

J.Q. ADAMS

"I am a man of reserved, cold, and forbidding manners."

SPEAKS

Every day, in good weather, President Adams would get up at 5 A.M.,

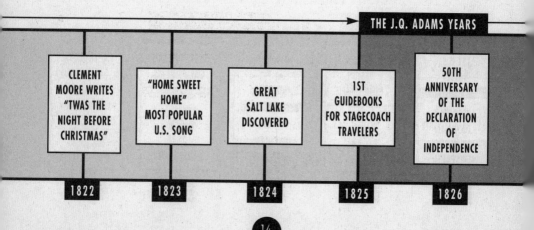

THE J.Q. ADAMS YEARS

CLEMENT MOORE WRITES "TWAS THE NIGHT BEFORE CHRISTMAS"	"HOME SWEET HOME" MOST POPULAR U.S. SONG	GREAT SALT LAKE DISCOVERED	1ST GUIDEBOOKS FOR STAGECOACH TRAVELERS	50TH ANNIVERSARY OF THE DECLARATION OF INDEPENDENCE
1822	1823	1824	1825	1826

walk down to Washington D.C.'s Potomac River, hang his clothes on a tree, and go for a swim. He was probably the only president to swim naked—at least in public!

Andrew Jackson

Andrew Jackson was the first "common" man to be elected. He was born in a rough-hewn log cabin in Waxhaw, South Carolina. His father died before he was born, and his oldest brother was killed while fighting for independence in the Continental Army. Andrew joined the army himself the following year, in 1780, but was soon captured and taken prisoner by the British. Later that same year, his mother died.

Patriotic Vocabulary

Democrat: Andrew Jackson formed the **Democratic Party** to show that he was a new type of candidate, drawing his support from poor, working-class people not usually involved in politics. The donkey became the symbol of the party when Jackson's opponents called him a "jackass" during the campaign.

After the war ended, Andrew Jackson made a name for himself, both as a lawyer and in the U.S. Army. He served as Tennessee's first representative in Congress, and led a volunteer army during the War of 1812.

7TH PRESIDENT
DEMOCRAT
1829–1837
BORN: MAR 15, 1767
DIED: JUNE 8, 1845

Andrew Jackson was a populist president. This meant he genuinely believed ordinary Americans— the farmers, pioneers, and shopkeepers—were what made the country strong. He felt they had enough common sense to

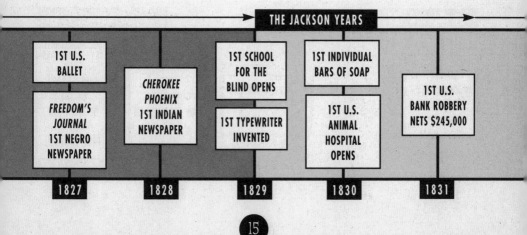

THE JACKSON YEARS

1ST U.S. BALLET

FREEDOM'S JOURNAL 1ST NEGRO NEWSPAPER

CHEROKEE PHOENIX 1ST INDIAN NEWSPAPER

1ST SCHOOL FOR THE BLIND OPENS

1ST TYPEWRITER INVENTED

1ST INDIVIDUAL BARS OF SOAP

1ST U.S. ANIMAL HOSPITAL OPENS

1ST U.S. BANK ROBBERY NETS $245,000

1827   1828   1829   1830   1831

make their own political decisions. This belief made him very popular, and later became known as "Jacksonian democracy."

At President Jackson's inauguration, a mob of more than 20,000 supporters followed his carriage from the Capitol to the White House, where the president opened the doors, and let the people in to celebrate.

Martin Van Buren

Martin Van Buren's interest in politics began at an early age. Every day after school, he helped at the Kinderhook, New York tavern, where his father worked. He loved to listen to the arguments and discussions of famous politicians who stopped by.

8TH PRESIDENT
DEMOCRAT
1837–1841
BORN: DEC 5, 1782
DIED: JULY 24, 1862

Van Buren had many jobs before he became president. He was a lawyer, country judge, state senator, secretary of state, minister to Great Britain, and vice-president under Andrew Jackson. As president, Van Buren led the United States during a very difficult time. In 1837, only two months after Van Buren took office, the country was

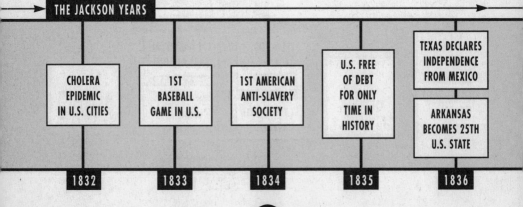

THE JACKSON YEARS

CHOLERA EPIDEMIC IN U.S. CITIES	1ST BASEBALL GAME IN U.S.	1ST AMERICAN ANTI-SLAVERY SOCIETY	U.S. FREE OF DEBT FOR ONLY TIME IN HISTORY	TEXAS DECLARES INDEPENDENCE FROM MEXICO / ARKANSAS BECOMES 25TH U.S. STATE
1832	1833	1834	1835	1836

struck by one of the worst economic depressions in history, a crisis that continued for the next ten years.

Some thought Van Buren behaved more like a king than a president, traveling in a fancy green coach, a kind of horse-drawn carriage, while the common people struggled. He was also a very stylish dresser, and was both praised and criticized for the expensive clothes he wore.

While some people thought him extravagant, the president had good ideas. He asked that an indepen-dent treasury be created to keep control of taxes collected. This plan was later adopted and is the basis for our treasury system today.

VAN BUREN

"As to the Presidency, the two happiest days of my life were those of my entrance upon the office and my surrender of it."

SPEAKS

William Henry Harrison

William Henry Harrison had a lot to say on his inaugural day. In fact, he delivered the longest inaugural speech ever—8,443 words! Unfortunately, after two hours spent standing outside in a very cold wind, he caught a serious cold.

The next day his cold developed into pneumonia. His doctors tried everything to cure him, even traditional Indian remedies and heated suction cups applied to his chest to draw out the disease. Nothing worked. In the end, he served the shortest term of any U.S. president, just thirty-one days. He was the first president to die in office.

9TH PRESIDENT
WHIG
1841
BORN: FEB 9, 1773
DIED: APR 4, 1841

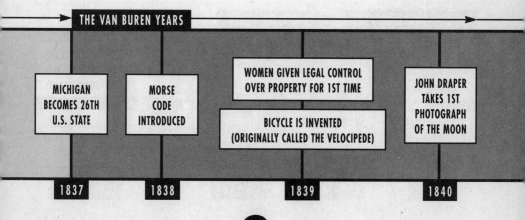

THE VAN BUREN YEARS

MICHIGAN BECOMES 26TH U.S. STATE

MORSE CODE INTRODUCED

WOMEN GIVEN LEGAL CONTROL OVER PROPERTY FOR 1ST TIME

BICYCLE IS INVENTED (ORIGINALLY CALLED THE VELOCIPEDE)

JOHN DRAPER TAKES 1ST PHOTOGRAPH OF THE MOON

1837 1838 1839 1840

William Henry Harrison had ten children and forty-eight grandchildren and great-grandchildren, far more than any other president. One of his grandchildren, Benjamin Harrison, went on to become the nation's 23rd president, a job that William Henry had won—but was unable to fulfill.

John Tyler

John Tyler was often called "His Accidency" because he was the first vice-president to become president upon the sudden death of William Henry Harrison. In fact, Tyler didn't even know the president was sick. He had returned home to Williamsburg, Virginia after the inauguration while the president was supposed to be selecting his Cabinet. Like the rest of the nation, Tyler was shocked by the news of the president's passing, and immediately

Patriotic Vocabulary

Whig: Led by Senators Daniel Webster and Henry Clay, the **Whig Party** believed in federal funding for roads, canals, and bridges, as well as a strong national bank. In 1856, many Whigs joined the new Republican Party, which was formed to oppose the spread of slavery.

10TH PRESIDENT
WHIG
1841–1845
BORN: MAR 29, 1790
DIED: JAN 18, 1862

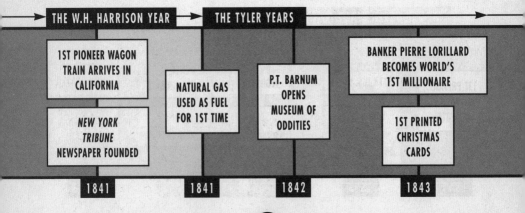

THE W.H. HARRISON YEAR → THE TYLER YEARS →

1ST PIONEER WAGON TRAIN ARRIVES IN CALIFORNIA

NEW YORK TRIBUNE NEWSPAPER FOUNDED

NATURAL GAS USED AS FUEL FOR 1ST TIME

P.T. BARNUM OPENS MUSEUM OF ODDITIES

BANKER PIERRE LORILLARD BECOMES WORLD'S 1ST MILLIONAIRE

1ST PRINTED CHRISTMAS CARDS

1841   1841   1842   1843

rode back to Washington, D.C. Less than a day later, John Tyler became America's tenth president.

Tyler was the first president whose wife died in office. Then he became the first president to marry while in office, wedding a twenty-three-year-old New York socialite named Julia Gardiner. He had a total of fifteen children, more than any other president. Tyler's youngest child was born when he was seventy years old. During his White House days, John Tyler threw a lot of parties for his children, grandchildren, and their friends. He sometimes even played the fiddle for them!

> **TYLER**
>
> "Take care that the laws be faithfully executed."
>
> **SPEAKS**

Many years after his presidency, John Tyler was elected to the Confederate House of Representatives, when the Southern states were trying to separate, or secede, from the Union. This made him the only president to be elected to two governments. As it happened, he died before his term in the rebel government could begin.

James Polk

When George Washington was elected president, it took many days for the news to spread. Word of James Polk's nomination for president, however, traveled fast. In fact, twenty minutes after the event, news of his nomination flashed to Washington, D.C. by telegraph. This

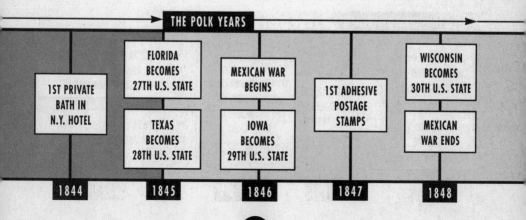

THE POLK YEARS

1844	1845	1846	1847	1848
1ST PRIVATE BATH IN N.Y. HOTEL	FLORIDA BECOMES 27TH U.S. STATE / TEXAS BECOMES 28TH U.S. STATE	MEXICAN WAR BEGINS / IOWA BECOMES 29TH U.S. STATE	1ST ADHESIVE POSTAGE STAMPS	WISCONSIN BECOMES 30TH U.S. STATE / MEXICAN WAR ENDS

was the first time the telegraph had been used in politics.

After Polk became president, the next bit of noteworthy news came from President Polk's inaugural ball. It was probably a festive spectacle, with lots of dancing and merrymaking . . . until the president and his wife arrived. Because of the First Lady's religious convictions, all dancing and music stopped when the Polks entered the room. In fact, no drinking or dancing were allowed at the White House during Polk's entire administration.

A former congressman, secretary of state, and governor of Tennessee, Polk served just one four-year term in the White House. He may have been one of the hardest-working presidents, for every day, from early morning until late into the evening, he worked to fulfill his campaign promises. In fact, Polk succeeded in delivering everything he had promised while campaigning. While in office, President Polk acquired new territories for the United States—land that would one day become California, New Mexico, Arizona, Nevada, Utah, and Wyoming.

> **11TH PRESIDENT**
> DEMOCRAT
> 1845–1849
> BORN: NOV 2. 1795
> DIED: JUNE 15. 1849

> **POLK**
> "I prefer to supervise the whole operation of government myself."
> **SPEAKS**

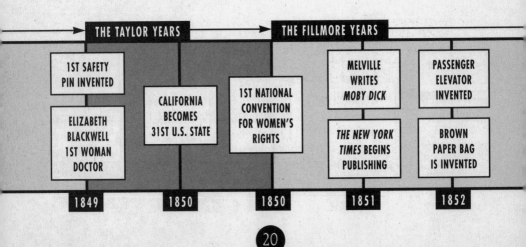

THE TAYLOR YEARS → THE FILLMORE YEARS

1ST SAFETY PIN INVENTED		1ST NATIONAL CONVENTION FOR WOMEN'S RIGHTS	MELVILLE WRITES *MOBY DICK*	PASSENGER ELEVATOR INVENTED
ELIZABETH BLACKWELL 1ST WOMAN DOCTOR	CALIFORNIA BECOMES 31ST U.S. STATE		*THE NEW YORK TIMES* BEGINS PUBLISHING	BROWN PAPER BAG IS INVENTED
1849	1850	1850	1851	1852

Zachary Taylor

While growing up in Kentucky, Zachary Taylor lived in daily danger from attacking Indian tribes. Living far from a city, he didn't have much schooling. At age twenty-four, Taylor chose a career in the military. He fought in the War of 1812, the Black Hawk War in 1832, and the Mexican War from 1846 to 1848. During the war against Mexico, he led America's troops to victory over superior Mexican forces and became a national hero. People everywhere began to talk about making Taylor president.

> **12TH PRESIDENT**
> **WHIG**
> **1849–1850**
> BORN: NOV 24, 1784
> DIED: JULY 9, 1850

But Zachary Taylor despised politics and politicians. He had never even voted in a presidential election! Nonetheless, in 1848, he found himself nominated for the presidency. As he was trained in the military to serve his nation, he felt it was his duty as an American to accept the nomination.

Taylor received many letters daily from people who admired him. In those days, it was customary for mail to be paid for by the person receiving it. Taylor refused most of the letters that came to him; otherwise, he would have gone broke!

Tragedy fell on Taylor early in his administration. After presiding at Fourth of July festivities one hot day, the president cooled off with a large serving of iced milk and

> **TAYLOR**
>
> "The idea that I should become President has never entered my head."
>
> **SPEAKS**

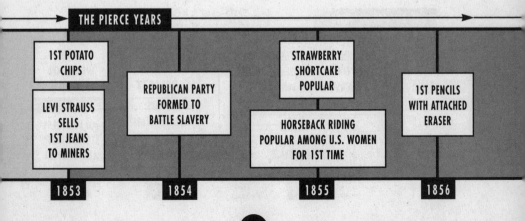

THE PIERCE YEARS

- 1ST POTATO CHIPS
- LEVI STRAUSS SELLS 1ST JEANS TO MINERS
- REPUBLICAN PARTY FORMED TO BATTLE SLAVERY
- STRAWBERRY SHORTCAKE POPULAR
- HORSEBACK RIDING POPULAR AMONG U.S. WOMEN FOR 1ST TIME
- 1ST PENCILS WITH ATTACHED ERASER

1853   **1854**   **1855**   **1856**

cherries. Later that night he developed severe cramps in his stomach. His doctors believed the snack had been infected with cholera, a deadly bacteria. Despite their best efforts, Zachary Taylor died five days later.

Millard Fillmore

Millard Fillmore was born in a log cabin and worked on his father's farm. Growing up, he attended a one-room schoolhouse and at age fifteen, apprenticed to become a clothmaker. In later years, Fillmore studied to become a lawyer and was elected to the New York state assembly. He went on to serve in the House of Representatives, and was elected vice-president under Zachary Taylor.

> **13TH PRESIDENT**
> **WHIG**
> **1850–1853**
> BORN: JAN 7, 1800
> DIED: MAR 8, 1874

Millard Fillmore was known as a poor speaker and an average leader, but he became vice-president because of his loyalty to the Whig Party. As was often the case, as vice-president he was excluded from any important role in the government (the vice-presidency is a largely ceremonial position). Then President Taylor died in office, and Fillmore became the nation's leader.

> **FILLMORE**
>
> "I had not the advantage of a classical education."
>
> **SPEAKS**

While in the White House, Millard Fillmore enjoyed some very new and modern conveniences.

THE BUCHANAN YEARS

PAUL MORPHY 1ST U.S. CHESS MASTER	PRESIDENT BUCHANAN SENDS MESSAGE TO ENGLAND'S QUEEN VICTORIA ON 1ST TRANSATLANTIC CABLE CONNECTING U.S. & EUROPE		CROQUET INTRODUCED IN U.S.
N.Y.C.'S CENTRAL PARK DESIGNED	MINNESOTA BECOMES 32ND U.S. STATE	OREGON BECOMES 33RD U.S. STATE	PONY EXPRESS BEGINS "FAST" MAIL DELIVERY
1857	**1858**	**1859**	**1860**

22

He was the first president to have a stove (until then, all cooking was done over open fireplaces) and the first to bathe in a White House bathtub with running water. He was also the first president to establish a permanent library in the presidential living quarters.

Franklin Pierce

The first president born in the 19th century, Pierce grew up in New Hampshire, where he became famous as a gifted trial lawyer. People came from all over just to hear him speak. In fact, he was such a skilled orator that President Pierce actually delivered his inaugural address from memory—all 3,319 words!

Upon hearing the news of Franklin Pierce's nomination for president, Jane Pierce, Franklin's wife, fainted. She hated politics and didn't want to become first lady. Franklin, in fact, had promised her that he wouldn't allow himself to be nominated for president. It was a promise he was not able to keep. At the 1852 Democratic Convention, when the delegates couldn't agree on a nominee, Pierce was chosen as a "compromise" candidate for the presidency. He had been unknown before that time.

14TH PRESIDENT
DEMOCRAT
1853–1857
BORN: NOV 23, 1804
DIED: OCT 8, 1869

The Pierce White House was a rather gloomy place. Two months before he was inaugurated as president, his only surviving son, Bennie,

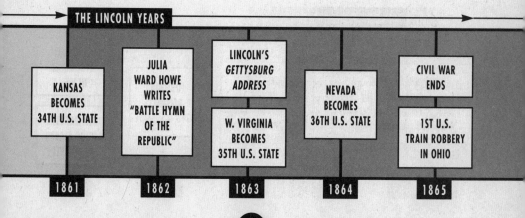

THE LINCOLN YEARS

KANSAS BECOMES 34TH U.S. STATE

JULIA WARD HOWE WRITES "BATTLE HYMN OF THE REPUBLIC"

LINCOLN'S GETTYSBURG ADDRESS

W. VIRGINIA BECOMES 35TH U.S. STATE

NEVADA BECOMES 36TH U.S. STATE

CIVIL WAR ENDS

1ST U.S. TRAIN ROBBERY IN OHIO

1861   1862   1863   1864   1865

was killed in a railroad accident (his two other sons had died earlier). Franklin Pierce served just one term as president, eager to end his unhappy years in the Oval Office.

James Buchanan

James Buchanan wanted very much to be president. He ran unsuccessfully for the Democratic presidential nomination in 1844, 1848, and 1852, and was finally elected to office in 1856.

Buchanan was a bachelor. Having vowed never to marry after the death of his fiancée many years before, he asked his niece, Miss Harriet Lane, if she would serve as official hostess at White House functions. Young Miss Lane, a tall elegant girl with strikingly beautiful eyes, did so well in this role that people soon considered her the most popular member of the Buchanan Administration. People wrote and dedicated songs to the pretty First Hostess, including the classic "Listen to the Mockingbird."

15TH PRESIDENT
DEMOCRAT
1857–1861
BORN: APR 23, 1791
DIED: JUNE 1, 1868

Buchanan was president at a very difficult time. The issue of slavery had divided the nation and the threat of Civil War loomed.

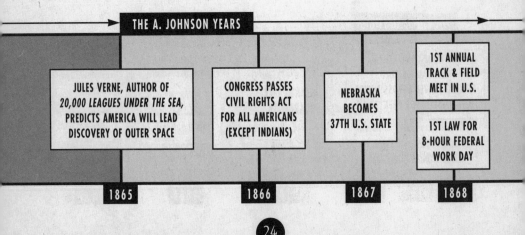

THE A. JOHNSON YEARS

JULES VERNE, AUTHOR OF *20,000 LEAGUES UNDER THE SEA*, PREDICTS AMERICA WILL LEAD DISCOVERY OF OUTER SPACE

CONGRESS PASSES CIVIL RIGHTS ACT FOR ALL AMERICANS (EXCEPT INDIANS)

NEBRASKA BECOMES 37TH U.S. STATE

1ST ANNUAL TRACK & FIELD MEET IN U.S.

1ST LAW FOR 8-HOUR FEDERAL WORK DAY

1865 1866 1867 1868

He gained so many enemies during his years in office that he left the White House unhappy and unwilling to try for a second term. When Abraham Lincoln succeeded him, Buchanan told him: "If you are as happy, my dear sir, on entering this house as I am in leaving it and returning home, you are the happiest man in the country."

BUCHANAN

"I, at least, meant well for my country."

SPEAKS

Abraham Lincoln

Abraham Lincoln was born in a one-room log cabin with a dirt floor. Although he had only one year of schoolhouse education, he taught himself to read and write. One of his favorite books was Parson Weem's biography of George Washington, which told stories of the first president's life while growing up.

Abraham Lincoln had many different jobs before he became president, from a ferryboat captain to a store clerk and a postmaster. By the age of thirty-five, he had become one of the best trial lawyers in the state

16TH PRESIDENT
REPUBLICAN
1861–1865
BORN: FEB 12, 1809
DIED: APR 15, 1865

of Illinois. But Lincoln never forgot his humble beginnings. He was famous for his folksy humor and straightforward way of speaking. Standing 6 feet, 4 inches, he was our tallest president and the first to wear a beard.

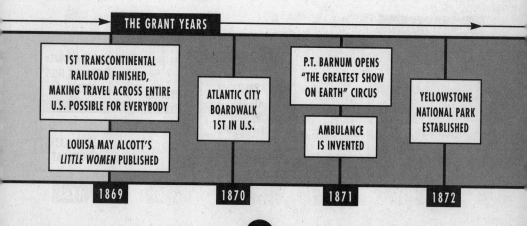

THE GRANT YEARS

1ST TRANSCONTINENTAL RAILROAD FINISHED, MAKING TRAVEL ACROSS ENTIRE U.S. POSSIBLE FOR EVERYBODY

P.T. BARNUM OPENS "THE GREATEST SHOW ON EARTH" CIRCUS

ATLANTIC CITY BOARDWALK 1ST IN U.S.

YELLOWSTONE NATIONAL PARK ESTABLISHED

LOUISA MAY ALCOTT'S *LITTLE WOMEN* PUBLISHED

AMBULANCE IS INVENTED

1869   1870   1871   1872

As president, Lincoln faced one of our nation's greatest challenges, the Civil War. He gained many enemies throughout the southern states—southerners who wanted to leave the Union and form a country of their own, called The Confederacy. President Lincoln fought hard to abolish slavery and to preserve the United States, even if it meant waging war against part of the nation he had been called upon to lead.

On April 14, 1865, while attending a play with his wife, Lincoln was shot and killed by a southerner named John Wilkes Booth. He was the first president to be assassinated. Lincoln is remembered as one of America's greatest presidents, for without him, the United States could have become two separate countries.

Andrew Johnson

Andrew Johnson had an unusual background for a man who would one day become president: his earlier years were neither military nor legal, and he never attended school. In fact, at age seventeen, it was Johnson's wife Eliza who taught him how to read and write. His

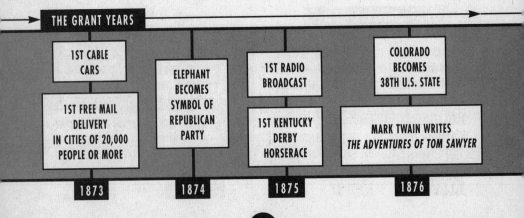

THE GRANT YEARS

| 1ST CABLE CARS | | | COLORADO BECOMES 38TH U.S. STATE |

| 1ST FREE MAIL DELIVERY IN CITIES OF 20,000 PEOPLE OR MORE | ELEPHANT BECOMES SYMBOL OF REPUBLICAN PARTY | 1ST RADIO BROADCAST | |

| | | 1ST KENTUCKY DERBY HORSERACE | MARK TWAIN WRITES *THE ADVENTURES OF TOM SAWYER* |

| 1873 | 1874 | 1875 | 1876 |

primary skills were as a tailor. He often made his own clothes, and when he became the Tennessee governor, almost thirty years later, he even made a suit for another governor.

Three hours after Lincoln's death, Johnson, newly appointed as vice-president for Lincoln's second term, was sworn in as president. He held the vice-presidency for forty-one days. The new president was faced with a difficult task: healing a divided country.

17TH PRESIDENT
NATIONAL UNION
1865–1869
BORN: DEC 29, 1808
DIED: JULY 31, 1875

Johnson believed that the country should abolish slavery. It was during Johnson's administration that the 15th Amendment to the Constitution was ratified, stating that the right to vote shall not be denied on account of race, color, or former slave status.

Like President Lincoln, Johnson's beliefs earned him many enemies. Because of his controversial policies, he was the first leader to be faced with impeachment—removal from office—by Congress. The specific charges held against him concerned the firing of a Cabinet member, but in fact he was opposed because of his

Patriotic Vocabulary

National Union: The **National Union Party** (also called the **Union Party**) was a name used by the Republican Party during the 1864 election. It was made up of Republicans and many Democrats who supported Lincoln's efforts to keep the nation together in the face of the Civil War.

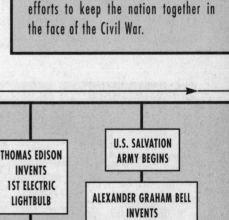

THE HAYES YEARS

1ST EASTER EGG HUNT AT WHITE HOUSE	THOMAS EDISON INVENTS PHONOGRAPH & RECORDS *MARY HAD A LITTLE LAMB* AS A DEMONSTRATION	THOMAS EDISON INVENTS 1ST ELECTRIC LIGHTBULB	U.S. SALVATION ARMY BEGINS
ROOT BEER IS INVENTED	1ST REGULAR TELEPHONE EXCHANGE		ALEXANDER GRAHAM BELL INVENTS 1ST WIRELESS PHONE
1877	**1878**	**1879**	**1880**

efforts to reunite the nation and grant rights to those who had been slaves before and during the Civil War. In the end, he was found not guilty by the margin of a single vote.

Ulysses S. Grant

Ulysses S. Grant was born Hiram Ulysses Grant, but changed it to Ulysses Hiram Grant because he didn't like the initials HUG. It wasn't the last time his name would be changed. When he was seventeen years old, Grant arrived at West Point to begin a military career. He was registered as Ulysses Simpson Grant due to a clerical error. He must have liked his newly appointed name, because he never changed it again!

Grant was a shy man who despised war and hated politics, yet he was known as one of the great Civil War heroes for the North. As President Lincoln's most trusted general, Grant led the Union armies to victory over the South. After the

18TH PRESIDENT
REPUBLICAN
1869–1877
BORN: APR 27, 1822
DIED: JULY 23, 1885

war, his fame and popularity swept him through two terms as president.

As with most men in the military, Grant spent much of his time on a horse. When he became president, his horses and ponies filled the White House

---

THE GARFIELD YEAR ◄─ THE ARTHUR YEARS

1ST COLOR PHOTOGRAPHS

CLARA BARTON FOUNDS NATIONAL SOCIETY OF THE RED CROSS

BANK ROBBER JESSE JAMES SHOT & KILLED BY MEMBER OF HIS OWN GANG

BOXING BECOMES POPULAR U.S. SPORT

LIFE MAGAZINE PUBLISHED

1881   1881   1882   1883

stables. He also loved to race through the streets of Washington. He was driving his presidential horse and buggy toward the White House one day when the horse's bridle was suddenly seized by William West, a police officer on patrol in that part of the city. West was about to arrest the speeding driver when the stunned and embarrassed officer realized it was none other than the president of the United States.

The patrolman apologized for the mistake, but President Grant insisted he receive a speeding ticket and commanded: "Officer, do your duty." The horse and buggy were impounded, and the president was forced to continue the rest of the way on foot.

> **GRANT**
>
> "I have never advocated war except as a means for peace."
>
> **SPEAKS**

Rutherford B. Hayes

Even as a young boy, Rutherford Hayes had his sights set on public office. He was successful in school, became a prosperous lawyer, a major general in the Civil War, and then governor of his home state of Ohio. Hayes won the presidency by a single electoral vote: 185 to 184. It was the closest electoral victory in America's history.

> **19TH PRESIDENT**
> REPUBLICAN
> 1877–1881
> BORN: OCT 4. 1822
> DIED: JAN 17. 1893

Traveling by train, Hayes was the first president to visit the West Coast of the United States. He was also

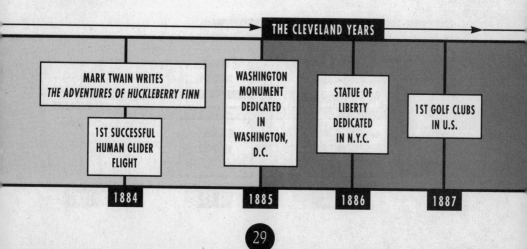

THE CLEVELAND YEARS

MARK TWAIN WRITES
THE ADVENTURES OF HUCKLEBERRY FINN

1ST SUCCESSFUL
HUMAN GLIDER
FLIGHT

WASHINGTON
MONUMENT
DEDICATED
IN
WASHINGTON,
D.C.

STATUE OF
LIBERTY
DEDICATED
IN N.Y.C.

1ST GOLF CLUBS
IN U.S.

1884   1885   1886   1887

the first to use a telephone in the White House.

Hayes and his wife Lucy were very religious, and held a daily prayer reading after breakfast. The First Family especially loved old-fashioned Sunday night hymn-singing, which became so popular that the vice-president, many of the president's Cabinet members, and even some congressmen often joined in!

James A. Garfield

James Garfield, the first left-handed president, graduated first in his class at Williams College in Massachusetts and later became a professor of Latin and Greek, then a college president at Western Reserve Eclectic Institute, a seminary in Chester, Ohio. In fact, his knowledge of languages came in handy while he was running for office: Garfield campaigned in both English and German, because it pleased the German-speaking immigrant population, and won him votes.

Few people believed Garfield would achieve much as president, because the Republican Party had become associated with the image of scandal, corrupt officials, and back-room deal-making during the previous two presidential administrations. Garfield proved he was different.

20TH PRESIDENT
REPUBLICAN
1881
BORN: NOV 31, 1831
DIED: SEPT 19, 1881

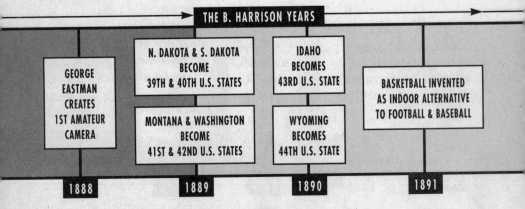

THE B. HARRISON YEARS

GEORGE EASTMAN CREATES 1ST AMATEUR CAMERA

N. DAKOTA & S. DAKOTA BECOME 39TH & 40TH U.S. STATES

MONTANA & WASHINGTON BECOME 41ST & 42ND U.S. STATES

IDAHO BECOMES 43RD U.S. STATE

WYOMING BECOMES 44TH U.S. STATE

BASKETBALL INVENTED AS INDOOR ALTERNATIVE TO FOOTBALL & BASEBALL

1888   1889   1890   1891

While in office he investigated wrongdoings in the post office and appointed government jobs on merit alone, something that had not been done in the past (traditionally civil service jobs had been given as rewards to those who supported the president).

President James Garfield served just 199 days in office. He was assassinated by a mentally ill man, Charles Guiteau, while walking through a Washington train station. Garfield lived ten weeks after the shooting, but ultimately, his doctors couldn't save him.

GARFIELD

"The President is the last person in the world to know what the people really want and think."

SPEAKS

Chester A. Arthur

Chester A. Arthur was president at the time of the first hot dogs and Buffalo Bill's Wild West shows. It was a rough-and-tumble time.

Few people believed Arthur belonged in the White House. A few years earlier he had been fired as collector of duties for the Port of New York when it was wrongly claimed that he had forced employees to contribute to Republican campaigns. Chester Arthur, however, was an honest and hard-working man, who, as president, sought to ban the corrupt traditions of the day. Possibly his most important achievement as president was the signing of the Pendleton Act, which reformed the civil

21ST PRESIDENT
REPUBLICAN
1881–1885
BORN: OCT. 5, 1829
DIED: NOV. 18, 1886

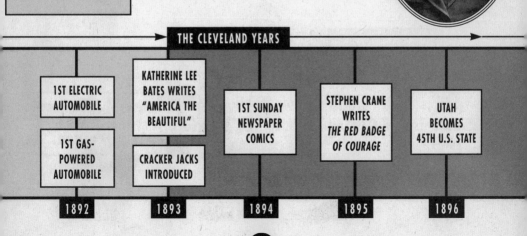

THE CLEVELAND YEARS

| 1ST ELECTRIC AUTOMOBILE | KATHERINE LEE BATES WRITES "AMERICA THE BEAUTIFUL" | 1ST SUNDAY NEWSPAPER COMICS | STEPHEN CRANE WRITES *THE RED BADGE OF COURAGE* | UTAH BECOMES 45TH U.S. STATE |

1ST GAS-POWERED AUTOMOBILE   CRACKER JACKS INTRODUCED

| 1892 | 1893 | 1894 | 1895 | 1896 |

service by creating competitive exams for government jobs.

Arthur was a well-dressed man who loved fine wine and good food and usually spent two to three hours at the dinner table. He loved elegant things, and when he became president, wasn't satisfied with the White House's traditional furniture. In fact, he refused to move into the mansion until the entire place was refurnished. He was also an avid fisherman, considered one of the best in America (his greatest catch was an eighty-pound bass!).

Grover Cleveland

Grover Cleveland was not very well-known before becoming president and was a virtual stranger in Washington. After years of working as a successful lawyer in Buffalo, New York, he was elected mayor of Buffalo, governor of New York, and then president of the United States within just three years time! His presidential inauguration drew the largest crowd Cleveland had ever seen.

Cleveland entered the White House determined to do well. At the beginning of his presidency, he wanted to do everything himself, even answer the White House telephones. He always studied

22ND PRESIDENT
DEMOCRAT
1885–1889

24TH PRESIDENT
1893–1897
BORN: MAR 18, 1837
DIED: JUNE 24, 1908

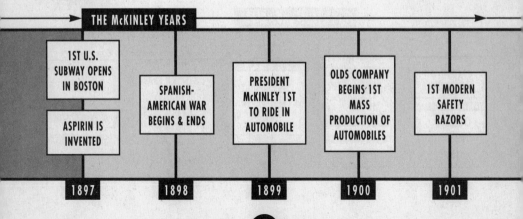

THE McKINLEY YEARS

1ST U.S. SUBWAY OPENS IN BOSTON				
ASPIRIN IS INVENTED	SPANISH-AMERICAN WAR BEGINS & ENDS	PRESIDENT McKINLEY 1ST TO RIDE IN AUTOMOBILE	OLDS COMPANY BEGINS 1ST MASS PRODUCTION OF AUTOMOBILES	1ST MODERN SAFETY RAZORS
1897	1898	1899	1900	1901

the task before him and often knew more about the issues of the day than the rest of his staff.

In 1886, at age forty-nine, Grover Cleveland wed twenty-one-year-old Frances Folsom. He was the first president married inside the White House, and she was the youngest first lady ever. He had known his young bride since her birth.

Cleveland was the only president to serve two non-consecutive terms. After losing the 1888 election to Benjamin Harrison, Cleveland beat Harrison in 1892. After being reelected, he inherited a deep economic depression, called the Panic of 1893. Unfortunately, much of the country blamed him for the worsening economy.

Grover Cleveland had five children. His daughter Esther was the first child born to a president in the White House (although John Tyler's granddaughter, Letitia, was the first child born in the White House). Cleveland's family did much to help the troubled president's popularity grow. His oldest daughter Ruth was so well-liked that she had a candy bar named after her—"Baby Ruth." The candy bar is still popular today.

> ## CLEVELAND
>
> "I am honest and sincere in my desire to do well."
>
> ## SPEAKS

Benjamin Harrison

Benjamin Harrison was sometimes called the "human iceberg." It wasn't that he

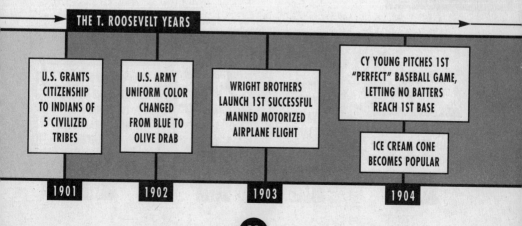

THE T. ROOSEVELT YEARS

U.S. GRANTS CITIZENSHIP TO INDIANS OF 5 CIVILIZED TRIBES	U.S. ARMY UNIFORM COLOR CHANGED FROM BLUE TO OLIVE DRAB	WRIGHT BROTHERS LAUNCH 1ST SUCCESSFUL MANNED MOTORIZED AIRPLANE FLIGHT	CY YOUNG PITCHES 1ST "PERFECT" BASEBALL GAME, LETTING NO BATTERS REACH 1ST BASE
			ICE CREAM CONE BECOMES POPULAR
1901	1902	1903	1904

23RD PRESIDENT
REPUBLICAN
1889–1893
BORN: AUG 20, 1833
DIED: MAR 13, 1901

was unfriendly, but he was a very formal man, and uncomfortable around other people. Still, his family had long been a part of American politics. His grandfather was William Henry Harrison, the nation's ninth president, and his great-grandfather, also named Benjamin Harrison, was a signer of the Declaration of Independence.

As president, Harrison was fortunate to have the support of Congress, which was made up of a majority of his fellow Republicans. Working with Congress, he followed through on a campaign promise to raise tariffs and protect American industry.

Harrison was the first president to use electricity in the White House, but it took some time. When lights were first installed, the president and his wife were so afraid of getting an electric shock they didn't turn them on for weeks! Then they were so afraid of touching the switches that they often went to sleep at night with all the house lights on.

Patriotic Vocabulary

Tariff: a fee or tax imposed by the government on imported or exported goods.

B. HARRISON

"The President is a good deal like the old camp horse; he is strapped up so he can't fall down."

SPEAKS

William McKinley

William McKinley had the distinction of being the last president of the 19th century. But his polit-

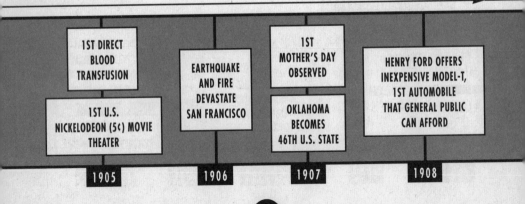

| 1ST DIRECT BLOOD TRANSFUSION | | 1ST MOTHER'S DAY OBSERVED | HENRY FORD OFFERS INEXPENSIVE MODEL-T, 1ST AUTOMOBILE THAT GENERAL PUBLIC CAN AFFORD |

1ST U.S. NICKELODEON (5¢) MOVIE THEATER

EARTHQUAKE AND FIRE DEVASTATE SAN FRANCISCO

OKLAHOMA BECOMES 46TH U.S. STATE

1905   1906   1907   1908

ical career began long before the turn of the century. Only eighteen years old, he enlisted as a private at the start of the Civil War, and was soon decorated for bravery in battle. His commander was Colonel Rutherford B. Hayes. After the war, McKinley helped Hayes win the election as governor of Ohio, and so began a political career of his own.

McKinley was a modern president, the first to campaign by telephone. He was also the first to use campaign buttons (in fact, he invented them!). It was an era of great growth and industry. McKinley supported American development and worked hard to ensure businesses could prosper with little government intervention.

McKINLEY

"Our differences are politics. Our agreements, principles."

SPEAKS

McKinley was also a devoted husband. His wife Ida suffered from epileptic seizures, so he insisted she be seated beside him at all state dinners, to be near him in case of a seizure. This was almost unheard of—traditionally, the first lady sits at the end of the table opposite the president.

During his second term, McKinley was attending a world fair, the 1901 Pan-American Exposition, when he was shot twice by an assassin. Even as he was dying, the president was thinking of Ida. "My wife," he said, "be careful how you tell her."

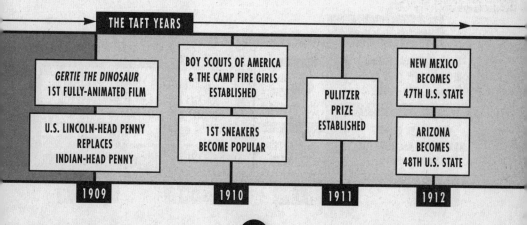

THE TAFT YEARS

| GERTIE THE DINOSAUR 1ST FULLY-ANIMATED FILM | BOY SCOUTS OF AMERICA & THE CAMP FIRE GIRLS ESTABLISHED | | NEW MEXICO BECOMES 47TH U.S. STATE |

U.S. LINCOLN-HEAD PENNY REPLACES INDIAN-HEAD PENNY

1ST SNEAKERS BECOME POPULAR

PULITZER PRIZE ESTABLISHED

ARIZONA BECOMES 48TH U.S. STATE

1909   1910   1911   1912

Theodore Roosevelt

Theodore Roosevelt was very sickly as a child, but grew up to become one of the most active presidents in U.S. history! Along with being president of the United States, Roosevelt was a rancher, explorer, historian, and author. His many hobbies included boxing, swimming, hunting, and mountain climbing. He loved to play games with his six children and take them on camping expeditions. At the end of a busy day in the White House, he would often sneak outside and run around the Washington Monument just to work off some of his extra energy.

Roosevelt was forty-two years old when he inherited the presidency, making him the youngest president in our nation's history. It was an era of new adventures, a time of new inventions. Theodore Roosevelt became the first president to ride in an automobile, the first to fly in an airplane, the first to ride in a submarine—even the first to publish a book! He also became the first president to win a Nobel Peace Prize after mediating peace in the 1904–1905 war between Russia and Japan.

Roosevelt enjoyed the presidency so much that he wanted to serve a third term in office. He formed a new political party called the Progressive or "Bull Moose" Party (it was named after

> **26TH PRESIDENT**
> REPUBLICAN
> 1901–1909
> BORN: OCT 27, 1858
> DIED: JAN 6, 1919

> ## T. ROOSEVELT
>
> "No president has ever enjoyed himself as much as I."
>
> **SPEAKS**

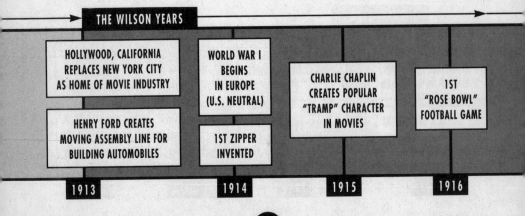

THE WILSON YEARS

HOLLYWOOD, CALIFORNIA REPLACES NEW YORK CITY AS HOME OF MOVIE INDUSTRY

WORLD WAR I BEGINS IN EUROPE (U.S. NEUTRAL)

CHARLIE CHAPLIN CREATES POPULAR "TRAMP" CHARACTER IN MOVIES

1ST "ROSE BOWL" FOOTBALL GAME

HENRY FORD CREATES MOVING ASSEMBLY LINE FOR BUILDING AUTOMOBILES

1ST ZIPPER INVENTED

1913   1914   1915   1916

Roosevelt declared himself "fit as a bull moose") and ran unsuccessfully for office in 1912.

William Howard Taft

William Howard Taft had big dreams for his future, but he never wanted to be president—instead, as a lawyer, he dreamed of being chief justice of the Supreme Court. After the presidency his wish was granted, and he became the only president who went on to serve in the judicial branch of the government.

During his presidency, President Taft was so tone deaf that he couldn't even recognize the national anthem when it was played! Still, he loved America. He was probably our country's best presidential baseball player. It was President Taft who started the tradition of throwing out the first baseball on opening day of the season on April 14, 1910, in a game between the Washington Senators and the Philadelphia Athletics.

> 27TH PRESIDENT
> REPUBLICAN
> 1909–1913
> BORN: SEPT 15, 1867
> DIED: MAR 8, 1930

Weighing in at 332 pounds, Taft was the heaviest president ever elected. He was so big, in fact, that he once got stuck in the White House bathtub. A new tub was ordered immediately, specially designed to fit the new president . . . or to hold *four* average-sized men!

> TAFT
>
> "Politics, when I am in it, makes me sick."
>
> SPEAKS

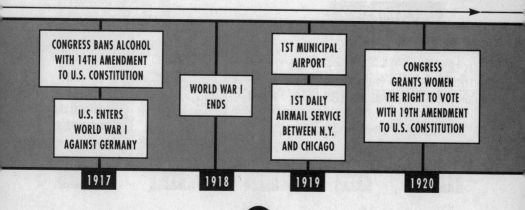

1917	1918	1919	1920
CONGRESS BANS ALCOHOL WITH 14TH AMENDMENT TO U.S. CONSTITUTION	WORLD WAR I ENDS	1ST MUNICIPAL AIRPORT	CONGRESS GRANTS WOMEN THE RIGHT TO VOTE WITH 19TH AMENDMENT TO U.S. CONSTITUTION
U.S. ENTERS WORLD WAR I AGAINST GERMANY		1ST DAILY AIRMAIL SERVICE BETWEEN N.Y. AND CHICAGO	

Woodrow Wilson

As a young boy, Woodrow Wilson was such a slow learner that he couldn't read until he was nine years old. Nonetheless, he went on to become the only president ever to earn a Ph.D., studying political science at Johns Hopkins University.

Wilson earned his doctorate degree by publishing a book called *Congressional Government*, which talked about how he believed the government should be run. He spent several years at Princeton, first as a professor, and then as president of the college. During this time he wrote many more books, including a history of America's people and George Washington's life story. These books made Wilson a very well-known and popular man. Many people thought Wilson would make a good president himself. Then, in 1912, he was elected to the White House.

During Wilson's first term in office, World War I raged in Europe. Wilson did not take sides in the war, and, in 1916, he was reelected with the slogan "He Kept Us Out of War." But then German submarines began to attack American ships. President Wilson decided the U.S. could remain neutral no longer. On April 2, 1917, he bravely led America and her allies to victory in Europe.

28TH PRESIDENT
DEMOCRAT
1913–1921
BORN: DEC 29, 1856
DIED: FEB 3, 1924

WILSON

"Sometimes people call me an idealist. Well, that is the way I know I am an American."

SPEAKS

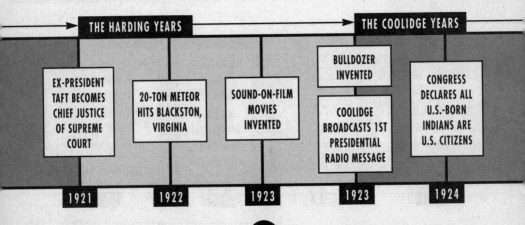

THE HARDING YEARS | THE COOLIDGE YEARS

EX-PRESIDENT TAFT BECOMES CHIEF JUSTICE OF SUPREME COURT	20-TON METEOR HITS BLACKSTON, VIRGINIA	SOUND-ON-FILM MOVIES INVENTED	BULLDOZER INVENTED / COOLIDGE BROADCASTS 1ST PRESIDENTIAL RADIO MESSAGE	CONGRESS DECLARES ALL U.S.-BORN INDIANS ARE U.S. CITIZENS
1921	1922	1923	1923	1924

Warren G. Harding

Warren G. Harding spent his childhood milking cows on his family's farm, but by the time he was nineteen he was ready for new challenges. He joined with two friends to buy a bankrupt Ohio newspaper called the *Marion Star* and soon took over the paper himself. Over several years Harding's newspaper became popular enough that the young publisher became well-known by many people. Such popularity prompted Harding to leave the newspaper business and launch a political career.

He discovered it was harder than he expected to be president. Harding was a nice man who hated to say no to others. He often had trouble taking sides on an issue. "I listen to one side and they seem right," he explained, "and then I talk to the other side and they seem just as right, and here I am where I started."

The people who worked for President Harding began to take advantage of his indecision, and reports circulated that many of his Cabinet members were corrupt. Harding decided to tour the nation to explain his policies to the American people and let them know he could be trusted. He called this tour the Voyage of Understanding. The trip

> **29TH PRESIDENT**
> **REPUBLICAN**
> **1921–1923**
> BORN: NOV 2, 1865
> DIED: AUG 2, 1923

HARDING

"I am not fit for this office and never should have been here."

SPEAKS

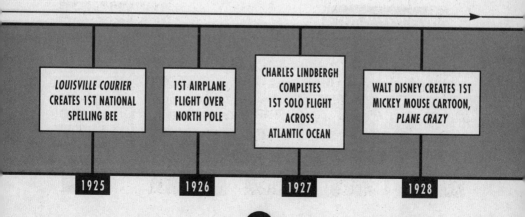

LOUISVILLE COURIER CREATES 1ST NATIONAL SPELLING BEE	1ST AIRPLANE FLIGHT OVER NORTH POLE	CHARLES LINDBERGH COMPLETES 1ST SOLO FLIGHT ACROSS ATLANTIC OCEAN	WALT DISNEY CREATES 1ST MICKEY MOUSE CARTOON, PLANE CRAZY
1925	1926	1927	1928

across the country exhausted the troubled president, however, and he died unexpectedly from a combination of apoplexy, pneumonia, and high blood pressure before he could finish the journey.

Calvin Coolidge

In college, Calvin Coolidge was often called "Silent Cal" because he was a man of few words. He liked it that way. He once said: "Four-fifths of all our troubles in this life would disappear if we would only sit down and keep still."

When Vice-President Coolidge received news about President Harding's death, he was visiting his father at his home in Vermont. Coolidge knelt down and said a prayer, and then arranged to have his father, who was a justice of the peace, administer the Presidential Oath. This made Coolidge the first and only president ever sworn in by his father!

He was also the first and only president whose picture was put on an American coin while he was still alive. The 1926 Sesquicentennial half-dollar had both Coolidge's and George Washington's faces on it. The president liked being represented on money, because he believed that America's

30TH PRESIDENT
REPUBLICAN
1923–1929
BORN: JULY 4, 1872
DIED: JAN 5, 1933

COOLIDGE

"The business of America is business."

SPEAKS

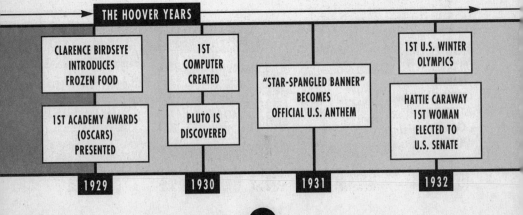

THE HOOVER YEARS

CLARENCE BIRDSEYE INTRODUCES FROZEN FOOD

1ST COMPUTER CREATED

1ST U.S. WINTER OLYMPICS

"STAR-SPANGLED BANNER" BECOMES OFFICIAL U.S. ANTHEM

1ST ACADEMY AWARDS (OSCARS) PRESENTED

PLUTO IS DISCOVERED

HATTIE CARAWAY 1ST WOMAN ELECTED TO U.S. SENATE

1929   1930   1931   1932

success was dependent on commerce and business.

After his first term in office, Coolidge decided not to run for reelection. To nobody's surprise, Silent Cal gave no explanation for his decision.

Herbert Hoover

Before any of the newly elected President Hoover's policies went into effect, the country's prosperity collapsed. A time of great financial panic, billions of dollars in business investments were lost overnight. The country had entered what was called the Great Depression.

> **31ST PRESIDENT**
> REPUBLICAN
> 1929–1933
> BORN: AUG 10, 1874
> DIED: OCT 20, 1964

President Hoover worked hard to reassure the American people and to solve the financial crisis, but the problems were too great to handle. When Hoover left the White House four years later, many people were out of work. The homeless who lived in piles of rubbish called their homes "Hoovervilles." Even the newspapers they used to cover themselves were called "Hoover blankets." Hoover had become the symbol of the Great Depression.

> **HOOVER**
>
> "The thing I enjoyed most were visits from children."
>
> **SPEAKS**

After his White House years, Hoover advised politicians and helped provide relief to Europe during World War II. When the war ended, he

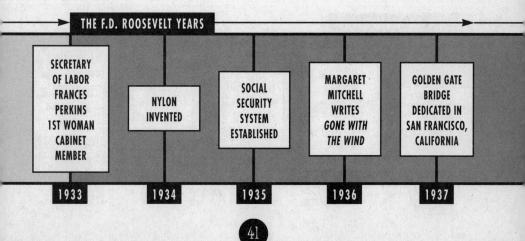

THE F.D. ROOSEVELT YEARS

SECRETARY OF LABOR FRANCES PERKINS 1ST WOMAN CABINET MEMBER	NYLON INVENTED	SOCIAL SECURITY SYSTEM ESTABLISHED	MARGARET MITCHELL WRITES *GONE WITH THE WIND*	GOLDEN GATE BRIDGE DEDICATED IN SAN FRANCISCO, CALIFORNIA
1933	1934	1935	1936	1937

served as chairman of relief organizations for Finland, Belgium, and Poland, three of America's allies. Hoover also coordinated food relief programs and led a study to improve and simplify the way the U.S. government worked.

When Hoover died in 1964, he had become one of the most-loved ex-presidents in American history. He had received fifty honorary degrees and more than seventy awards and medals. Even the first asteroid named for a president was called "Hooveria."

Franklin Delano Roosevelt

Franklin Delano Roosevelt was born to serve his nation. His ancestors had been pilgrims on the *Mayflower*, and his bloodline connected him to eleven former American presidents: George Washington, John Adams, James Madison, John Quincy Adams, Martin Van Buren, William Henry Harrison, Zachary Taylor, U.S. Grant, Benjamin Harrison, Theodore Roosevelt, and William Howard Taft!

Roosevelt was elected president twenty-four years after his famous cousin Theodore Roosevelt had left the White House. Unlike Theodore Roosevelt, Franklin did not have the advantage of boundless physical energy. In 1920, he had contracted polio, a disease which paralyzed his legs and forced him to wear leg braces or use a wheelchair for the rest of his life.

Despite his handicap, FDR was considered by many to be among

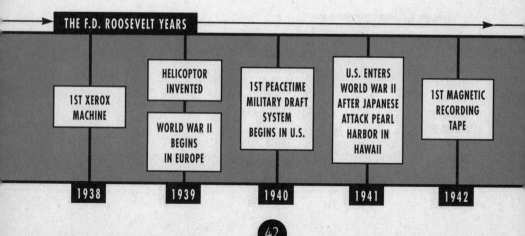

THE F.D. ROOSEVELT YEARS

1ST XEROX MACHINE	HELICOPTOR INVENTED / WORLD WAR II BEGINS IN EUROPE	1ST PEACETIME MILITARY DRAFT SYSTEM BEGINS IN U.S.	U.S. ENTERS WORLD WAR II AFTER JAPANESE ATTACK PEARL HARBOR IN HAWAII	1ST MAGNETIC RECORDING TAPE
1938	1939	1940	1941	1942

our finest leaders and greatest presidents. He helped our country survive its two greatest perils in the twentieth century, the Great Depression and World War II. He was America's longest serving president, holding almost four full terms in office.

32ND PRESIDENT
DEMOCRAT
1933–1945
BORN: JAN 30, 1882
DIED: APR 12, 1945

Soon after his death, Congress passed a law that allows presidents no more than two consecutive terms in office. Although few regret Roosevelt's many years of leadership, it was decided that the power of the presidency should never be in a single person's hands for that long again.

F.D. ROOSEVELT

"The fate of America cannot depend upon any one man."

SPEAKS

Harry S Truman

Harry S Truman never wanted to be president, but he was asked to serve as vice-president by Franklin Roosevelt while the president was running for his fourth term in office. America was in the midst of a war and Truman, who had been a colonel in World War I, felt a sense of patriotic duty that told him he couldn't say no. When FDR died suddenly in 1945, Truman went on to lead America to victory in World War II.

33RD PRESIDENT
DEMOCRAT
1945–1953
BORN: MAY 8, 1884
DIED: DEC 26, 1972

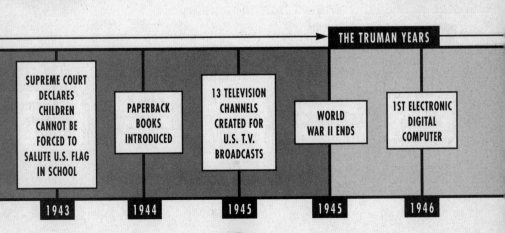

THE TRUMAN YEARS

SUPREME COURT DECLARES CHILDREN CANNOT BE FORCED TO SALUTE U.S. FLAG IN SCHOOL	PAPERBACK BOOKS INTRODUCED	13 TELEVISION CHANNELS CREATED FOR U.S. T.V. BROADCASTS	WORLD WAR II ENDS	1ST ELECTRONIC DIGITAL COMPUTER
1943	1944	1945	1945	1946

Truman was president at a time when there were many new inventions. He was the first president to address the American people on television from the White House, and the first to tape-record his press conferences.

Many people wonder what the "S" in Truman's middle name stands for, and why there is no period after the initial. In fact, it doesn't stand for any one name at all. The letter was chosen by his parents to honor relatives whose names start with "s" on both sides of the family. Truman was devoted to his own family, and spent so much time with his wife Bess and daughter Margaret, that the three became known as "The Three Musketeers!"

Dwight D. Eisenhower

Dwight David Eisenhower was one of the greatest military leaders in American history. He entered the U.S. Military Academy after high school and went on to become a four-star general, leading the U.S. military and its allies to victory in Europe in World War II.

People everywhere adopted the slogan "I like Ike," and like him they did: Eisenhower became a very popular hero in America and was elected president soon after he resigned from the military.

34TH PRESIDENT
REPUBLICAN
1953–1961
BORN: OCT 14, 1890
DIED: MAR 28, 1969

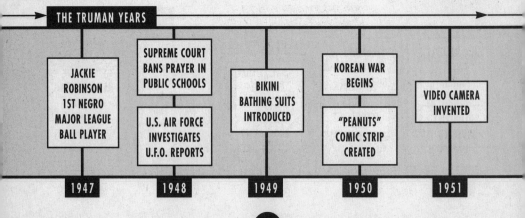

THE TRUMAN YEARS

1947	1948	1949	1950	1951
JACKIE ROBINSON 1ST NEGRO MAJOR LEAGUE BALL PLAYER	SUPREME COURT BANS PRAYER IN PUBLIC SCHOOLS / U.S. AIR FORCE INVESTIGATES U.F.O. REPORTS	BIKINI BATHING SUITS INTRODUCED	KOREAN WAR BEGINS / "PEANUTS" COMIC STRIP CREATED	VIDEO CAMERA INVENTED

Eisenhower was president during a time when many Americans felt hopeful about the future. Hawaii and Alaska joined the United States during this time, making Eisenhower the first president to serve all fifty states.

Ike loved to play golf and even added a putting green on the White House lawn where he could relax and solve presidential problems while he practiced his game.

> **EISENHOWER**
>
> "The future of this republic is in the hands of the American voter."
>
> **SPEAKS**

John F. Kennedy

John Fitzgerald Kennedy was born the second son in a family where it was hoped that the oldest boy would one day become president. He commanded a torpedo boat in World War II, and became a hero after saving the lives of his crew. When his older brother Joe was killed in the war, JFK carried on the family dream and entered politics himself.

One year later, at age twenty-nine, he was elected to Congress. Kennedy traveled widely and became very popular, famous for his sense of humor and good looks. In 1952, he became a Senator and then, in 1960, at age forty-three, he was elected president.

35TH PRESIDENT
DEMOCRAT
1961–1963
BORN: MAY 29, 1917
DIED: NOV 22, 1963

The new president's optimism and energy inspired many people throughout the nation. In 1961, Kennedy formed the Peace Corps, in which Americans

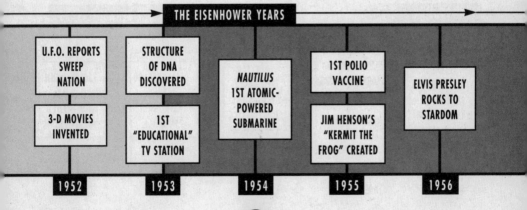

THE EISENHOWER YEARS

U.F.O. REPORTS SWEEP NATION	STRUCTURE OF DNA DISCOVERED	*NAUTILUS* 1ST ATOMIC-POWERED SUBMARINE	1ST POLIO VACCINE	ELVIS PRESLEY ROCKS TO STARDOM
3-D MOVIES INVENTED	1ST "EDUCATIONAL" TV STATION		JIM HENSON'S "KERMIT THE FROG" CREATED	
1952	**1953**	**1954**	**1955**	**1956**

could travel the world and help other people lead better lives. Since then, more than 150,000 people have traveled to nearly 100 countries to help fulfill JFK's vision.

Kennedy was the only president ever awarded a Pulitzer Prize, after writing *Profiles in Courage*, a book about the lives of great American leaders. Then, in November of 1963, Kennedy became the fourth American president to be assassinated. His sudden death shocked and saddened the entire world, and the controversy over his death still lingers today.

Lyndon B. Johnson

Lyndon Johnson became America's president when John F. Kennedy was assassinated. The two men shared many of the same goals for the nation, but in many ways they were very different. While JFK had been wealthy, Johnson was the son of a poor farmer, who worked as a shoeshine boy in his youth. Kennedy was famous for his sophistication; Johnson was more of a cowboy who preferred a cook-out to a formal White House dinner.

In important ways, however, President Johnson carried on the vision JFK had inspired. Among his various

36TH PRESIDENT
DEMOCRAT
1963–1969
BORN: AUG 27, 1908
DIED: JAN 22, 1973

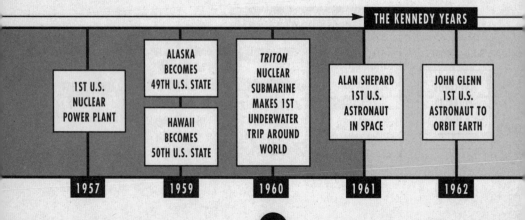

THE KENNEDY YEARS

1ST U.S. NUCLEAR POWER PLANT	ALASKA BECOMES 49TH U.S. STATE	TRITON NUCLEAR SUBMARINE MAKES 1ST UNDERWATER TRIP AROUND WORLD	ALAN SHEPARD 1ST U.S. ASTRONAUT IN SPACE	JOHN GLENN 1ST U.S. ASTRONAUT TO ORBIT EARTH
	HAWAII BECOMES 50TH U.S. STATE			
1957	1959	1960	1961	1962

successes were a Civil Rights Act and a Voting Rights Act, outlawing discrimination against minorities. He also created Medicare programs that helped poor people pay their medical bills.

Johnson served at a time when many young people questioned the authority of America's leaders, and protested the country's involvement in the Vietnam War.

After six long years in office, he surprised everyone by announcing that he would not seek another term in the White House.

> **L.B. JOHNSON**
>
> "There are no problems that we cannot solve together."
>
> **SPEAKS**

Richard M. Nixon

Richard Nixon was raised to believe that hard work could make the difference between success and failure in all things. Born to a working-class family in Yorba Linda, California, he was a quiet, serious student, studying hard to achieve good grades. After serving in World War II, he set his sights on becoming a Congressman. Working hard, Nixon won the election to the U.S. House of Representatives (representing California) by 15,000 votes.

> **37TH PRESIDENT**
> REPUBLICAN
> 1969–1974
> BORN: JAN 9, 1913
> DIED: APR 22, 1994

Once in Washington, Nixon emerged as a hard fighter against what was seen as a threat to the "American

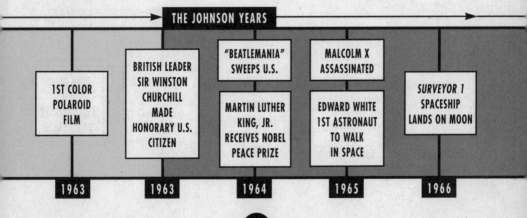

THE JOHNSON YEARS

1ST COLOR POLAROID FILM	BRITISH LEADER SIR WINSTON CHURCHILL MADE HONORARY U.S. CITIZEN	"BEATLEMANIA" SWEEPS U.S. / MARTIN LUTHER KING, JR. RECEIVES NOBEL PEACE PRIZE	MALCOLM X ASSASSINATED / EDWARD WHITE 1ST ASTRONAUT TO WALK IN SPACE	SURVEYOR 1 SPACESHIP LANDS ON MOON
1963	1963	1964	1965	1966

way" of life—communism. In 1950, he was elected to the Senate, and then, in 1952, Eisenhower chose Nixon as his running mate.

Years later, in 1968, after he was first defeated by JFK, Nixon was elected president himself. After years of talking about the evils of communism, he surprised everybody by signing friendship treaties with the world's two greatest communist countries, China and the Soviet Union. But the U.S. was still at war with communism in Vietnam, and the American people demanded an end to the war. Running for reelection, Nixon promised peace was at hand.

But then five men tied to Nixon were caught breaking into the Democratic campaign headquarters at Washington, D.C.'s Watergate Hotel. Suspicions turned toward the president, although he denied any knowledge of this illegal activity.

Two years later Congress began impeachment proceedings. Rather than face impeachment, Richard Nixon became the first president ever to resign from the White House.

Gerald R. Ford

Gerald Ford was the only president adopted as a child. He made friends easily, and was a star athlete on the baseball, basketball, and football teams in high school. At the University of Michigan, he was named most valuable player, and received offers to play profes-

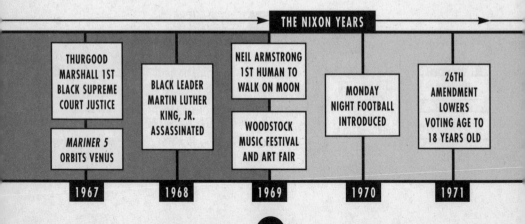

THE NIXON YEARS

| THURGOOD MARSHALL 1ST BLACK SUPREME COURT JUSTICE | BLACK LEADER MARTIN LUTHER KING, JR. ASSASSINATED | NEIL ARMSTRONG 1ST HUMAN TO WALK ON MOON | MONDAY NIGHT FOOTBALL INTRODUCED | 26TH AMENDMENT LOWERS VOTING AGE TO 18 YEARS OLD |

MARINER 5 ORBITS VENUS

WOODSTOCK MUSIC FESTIVAL AND ART FAIR

1967   1968   1969   1970   1971

sional football. But Ford had another dream—to become a lawyer.

After serving in World War II, he decided to run for Congress. Nobody gave him much chance of winning against Bartel Jankman, a popular Washington incumbent, but Ford campaigned in a very straightforward, personal way. He spent each day meeting people in his district, pitching hay with farmers, or shaking hands with downtown shoppers. This simple approach appealed to voters, and he won the election by a large margin.

Once in Washington, Ford became a well-liked member of the House. When a financial scandal forced Vice-President Agnew to resign in 1973, President Nixon selected the honest and trusted Ford as his replacement. When Nixon himself was forced to resign, Gerald Ford became president and led the country for the remainder of Nixon's term.

38TH PRESIDENT
REPUBLICAN
1974–1977
BORN: JULY 14, 1913

FORD

"In America, anyone can be president."

SPEAKS

Jimmy Carter

At age five, young Jimmy could be found selling boiled peanuts on the streets of his hometown, Plaines, Georgia. Eventually, he took over his father's farming business. He went on to serve as chairman of a local county school board, and discovered he enjoyed the

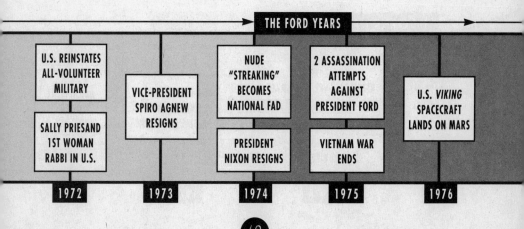

THE FORD YEARS

U.S. REINSTATES ALL-VOLUNTEER MILITARY

SALLY PRIESAND 1ST WOMAN RABBI IN U.S.

VICE-PRESIDENT SPIRO AGNEW RESIGNS

NUDE "STREAKING" BECOMES NATIONAL FAD

PRESIDENT NIXON RESIGNS

2 ASSASSINATION ATTEMPTS AGAINST PRESIDENT FORD

VIETNAM WAR ENDS

U.S. *VIKING* SPACECRAFT LANDS ON MARS

1972   1973   1974   1975   1976

give-and-take of politics. He set his sights on the Georgia state senate, then the governorship. Almost overnight, a peanut farmer from an unknown town in a small state found himself elected to the highest office in the land—the presidency.

39TH PRESIDENT
DEMOCRAT
1977–1981
BORN: OCT 1, 1924

Jimmy set a different tone for his presidency from the outset, choosing to walk down the short parade route at his inauguration instead of riding in the traditional presidential limousine. Human rights and world peace were very important to Carter, who mediated a peace treaty between Israel and Egypt after thirty years of war. Then, during the last year of his presidency, Islamic militants took over the U.S. Embassy in Iran and held the Americans there hostage. Unable to win their release, President Carter also found himself unable to win reelection to the Oval Office.

CARTER

"If I ever tell a lie, I want you to come and take me out of the White House."

SPEAKS

Ronald Reagan

Ronald Reagan won the presidency during a time when many Americans felt uncertain that the world's leaders could help solve their problems. "Government is not the solution to our problems," he said. "Government is the problem." Reagan made people feel good about

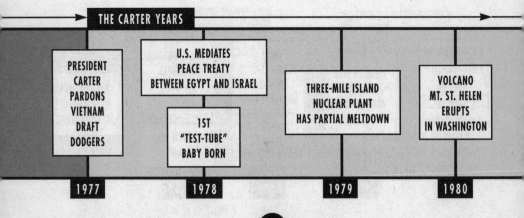

THE CARTER YEARS

| PRESIDENT CARTER PARDONS VIETNAM DRAFT DODGERS | U.S. MEDIATES PEACE TREATY BETWEEN EGYPT AND ISRAEL | | | |
| | | 1ST "TEST-TUBE" BABY BORN | THREE-MILE ISLAND NUCLEAR PLANT HAS PARTIAL MELTDOWN | VOLCANO MT. ST. HELEN ERUPTS IN WASHINGTON |

| 1977 | 1978 | 1979 | 1980 |

being Americans again. He had a simple, old-fashioned way of making people feel hopeful about the future.

Before entering politics, Reagan was a movie star. He played American heroes, tough guys, and cowboys in many of his pictures. It was an image he carried over to his political career. Because of his experience speaking in front of cameras and his ability to project just the right image, President Reagan was often called "The Great Communicator." At age sixty-nine, he was the oldest person ever elected president.

40TH PRESIDENT
REPUBLICAN
1981—1989
BORN: FEB 6, 1911

REAGAN

"Freedom
is the right
of all human
beings."

SPEAKS

In 1981, he was shot by John Hinkley, Jr., a mentally ill young man, but the president survived. "I just forgot to duck," Reagan explained with a smile.

Reagan's cheerful optimism inspired hope around the world. Many people believe that Reagan made it possible for many formerly communist countries in Eastern Europe to become free nations. Reagan ended his two terms in office as one of the most popular presidents in modern times.

George Bush

George Bush was born to a wealthy family, and was raised to believe in public service as a way of repaying the country for the good

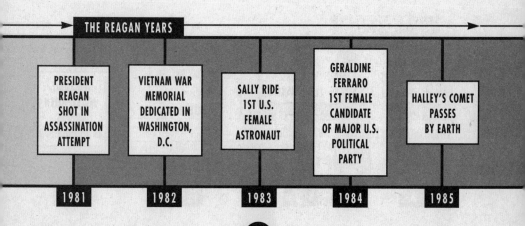

THE REAGAN YEARS

| PRESIDENT REAGAN SHOT IN ASSASSINATION ATTEMPT | VIETNAM WAR MEMORIAL DEDICATED IN WASHINGTON, D.C. | SALLY RIDE 1ST U.S. FEMALE ASTRONAUT | GERALDINE FERRARO 1ST FEMALE CANDIDATE OF MAJOR U.S. POLITICAL PARTY | HALLEY'S COMET PASSES BY EARTH |
| 1981 | 1982 | 1983 | 1984 | 1985 |

things given him. He was always considered a gentleman—a nice man who had a long list of friends and acquaintances. When Bush entered politics, his friends were willing to help him succeed—and succeed he did.

41ST PRESIDENT
REPUBLICAN
1989–1993
BORN: JUNE 12, 1924

During World War II, George Bush was the youngest navy pilot to fly combat over the Pacific Ocean. For his many heroic missions, he was awarded the Distinguished Flying Cross. After the war, Bush decided not to join his family as a banker, but moved to Texas, where he became rich investing in oil. The state elected the popular young tycoon to Congress. Soon after that, he became America's ambassador to the United Nations before being elected president.

BUSH

"We have had triumphs, we have had mistakes."

SPEAKS

President Bush served the nation at a time when freedom and democracy were spreading around the world. He called this change the "New World Order." When the small, militant middle eastern country of Iraq invaded its neighboring country Kuwait, Bush organized "Operation Desert Storm," a coalition of nations to repel the attack, and restore freedom to the area. Operation Desert Storm was successful in re-liberating Kuwait and was seen as a test of Bush's New World Order, making him popular in America and around the world.

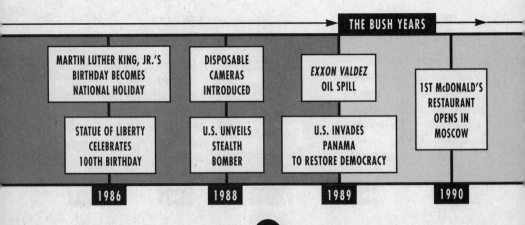

THE BUSH YEARS

MARTIN LUTHER KING, JR.'S BIRTHDAY BECOMES NATIONAL HOLIDAY

DISPOSABLE CAMERAS INTRODUCED

EXXON VALDEZ OIL SPILL

1ST McDONALD'S RESTAURANT OPENS IN MOSCOW

STATUE OF LIBERTY CELEBRATES 100TH BIRTHDAY

U.S. UNVEILS STEALTH BOMBER

U.S. INVADES PANAMA TO RESTORE DEMOCRACY

1986   1988   1989   1990

Bill Clinton

Bill Clinton was the first president elected from the generation born after World War II, often called the "Baby Boomers." Like many others his age, he grew up in a time when young people questioned the honesty of the president and protested America's involvement in the Vietnam War.

> **42ND PRESIDENT**
> DEMOCRAT
> 1993—
> BORN: AUG 19, 1946

In 1963, as part of an American Legion group called Boy's Nation, Clinton was given the opportunity to visit the White House, and shook hands with President Kennedy. He was impressed by the president, and decided that he wanted to become president himself one day.

Fifteen years later, at age thirty-two, he was elected governor in his home state of Arkansas. Then, in 1993, his boyhood wish was granted when Bill Clinton became our nation's 42nd president.

Clinton was the first president to have been a Rhodes Scholar, a very high academic honor. Like his hero, President Kennedy, Clinton works to promote greater peace in the world and equality among all Americans. In 1993, he helped mediate a historic peace treaty between long-time middle eastern enemies Israel and the Palestine Liberation Organization (PLO).

> **CLINTON**
>
> "There is nothing wrong with America that cannot be cured by what is right with America."
>
> **SPEAKS**

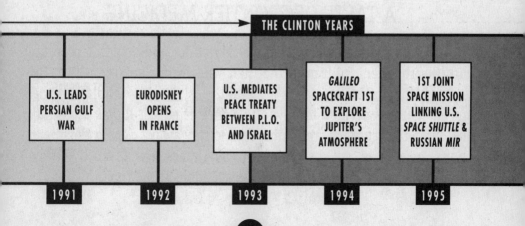

THE CLINTON YEARS

U.S. LEADS PERSIAN GULF WAR	EURODISNEY OPENS IN FRANCE	U.S. MEDIATES PEACE TREATY BETWEEN P.L.O. AND ISRAEL	GALILEO SPACECRAFT 1ST TO EXPLORE JUPITER'S ATMOSPHERE	1ST JOINT SPACE MISSION LINKING U.S. SPACE SHUTTLE & RUSSIAN MIR
1991	1992	1993	1994	1995

Benjamin Harrison often visited his grandfather, President William Henry Harrison, in the White House. John Quincy Adams traveled with his father, President John Adams, to Europe. Most of America's presidents, however, spent their childhoods thinking of anything *but* the presidency . . . leading lives just like any other American kid.

A PROMISE IS A PROMISE

As a youngster, Jefferson used to play under a favorite oak with his best friend, Dabney Carr. The two boys promised each other that when they died, they would both be buried under the tree. Dabney died some years later, while Jefferson was away in Europe, and was buried in the local cemetery. Remembering their boyhood promise, Jefferson had Dabney's bones retrieved and reburied under the oak tree (which was then part of his Monticello estate) as planned.

Many years later, in keeping with his last request, the president himself was buried under the old oak tree, as were the rest of his family members. And so a boyhood promise was fulfilled.

A TASTE OF FRONTIER MEDICINE

Ten-year-old James Polk was a sickly child, and couldn't keep up with the rougher children of the then wild frontier of Tennessee. He suffered from gallstones, large mineral deposits in his gallbladder. He and his parents decided to have the stones removed. It was a painful and dangerous surgery, and James had to stay awake during the operation. So, to ease the discomfort, young James was given a steady supply of alcohol, the only anesthesia available at the time.

THE BOY WHO SAT TO SLEEP

As a boy, Theodore Roosevelt didn't have to go to bed—but this didn't make him very happy. Why? Sick Teddy suffered from asthma. And, because of his asthma, he often had to sleep sitting in a chair. It was the only way he could stop coughing!

FRANKLIN COLLECTS STAMPS

Franklin Delano Roosevelt, our nation's 32nd president, liked to collect stamps. From the time he was eleven years old, he managed to save more than 25,000 stamps in forty albums. He even suggested designs for new stamps while serving as president! After his death, his presidential collection sold for $200,000.

LYNDON RUNS AWAY FROM HOME

When he was fifteen years old, Lyndon B. Johnson ran away from his home in Johnson City, Texas. The future congressman, senator, and president made his way to California, working as an auto mechanic and grape picker in the vineyards. After several months, he returned home and worked odd jobs before entering Southwest Texas State Teachers College in 1927.

DAD FORCES JIMMY TO WEAR GIRL'S SHOES

When Jimmy Carter was still in high school, his dad forced him to wear women's high-button shoes. Why? As the story goes, his father, who owned a general convenience store, found he had more women's high-button shoes on hand than he could possibly hope to sell. Thus, he decided that every member of the family should wear them to reduce his supply.

The Presidents' Birthplaces

To be qualified for the position of president, you must be born in the United States. Amazingly enough, half of the presidents were born in only four states! Which four were they?*

Washington	Virginia	Cleveland	New Jersey
John Adams	Massachusetts	B. Harrison	Ohio
Jefferson	Virginia	McKinley	Ohio
Madison	Virginia	T. Roosevelt	New York
Monroe	Virginia	Taft	Ohio
J.Q. Adams	Massachusetts	Wilson	Virginia
Jackson	S. Carolina	Harding	Ohio
Van Buren	New York	Coolidge	Vermont
W.H. Harrison	Virginia	Hoover	Iowa
Tyler	Virginia	F.D. Roosevelt	New York
Polk	N. Carolina	Truman	Missouri
Taylor	Virginia	Eisenhower	Texas
Fillmore	New York	Kennedy	Massachusetts
Pierce	New Hampshire	L.B. Johnson	Texas
Buchanan	Pennsylvania	Nixon	California
Lincoln	Kentucky	Ford	Nebraska
A. Johnson	N. Carolina	Carter	Georgia
Grant	Ohio	Reagan	Illinois
Hayes	Ohio	Bush	Massachusetts
Garfield	Ohio	Clinton	Arkansas
Arthur	Vermont		

Early Adventures

Sometimes when we think of our presidents, we forget that they actually had lives before the American people elected them to lead the nation. Each of our leaders have stories to tell from their early days.

FROM SERVANT . . . TO PRESIDENT

Many of America's presidents have come from very humble beginnings, so humble, in fact, that two of our leaders began life as servants. As children, both Millard Fillmore and Andrew Johnson signed on as apprentices to learn a trade. They entered an indentured servitude, a kind of "contract" labor in which a master "owned" the apprentice for five to seven years. During that contracted period of time, life for the apprentice was not much different than being a slave.

Neither boy enjoyed this type of life—can you blame them? Andrew Johnson ran away from the tailor to whom he was indentured. Millard Fillmore, indentured to a clothmaker, was finally able to buy his early freedom after saving thirty dollars.

THE UNION & CONFEDERACY
UNITED BY MARRIAGE?

Unbelievable as it seems, Jefferson Davis, president of the Confederacy during the Civil War, was once married to the daughter of President Zachary Taylor, who believed in the Union cause!

In 1832, Jefferson Davis, a recent graduate of West Point Military Academy, met and fell in love with Sarah Knox, whose father was his post commander—and a future president of the United States. Zachary Taylor didn't want his daughter married to "a military man," and forbade them to wed. But when Sarah was of legal age, she and Jefferson ignored his wishes, and married anyway.

It's impossible to know how America's history might have been written differently had Sarah not died three months later from a malarial fever. As it was, the two men grew further apart, leading to the day when Davis, elected to lead the Confederate States of America, led the battle to divide the young nation into two separate countries.

ABRAHAM LINCOLN'S SECRET FILING SYSTEM

Before Abraham Lincoln was elected to the presidency, he shared an Illinois law practice with a man named William Herndon. As Mr. Herndon explains in his book *Life of Lincoln*, the future president had a secret system for finding important papers on his often-messy desk:

"Lincoln had always on the top of our desk a bundle of papers into which he slipped anything he wished to keep and afterwards refer to.

Did You Know

... WASHINGTON CROSSED THE DELAWARE IN GERMANY?

Emanuel Leutze's famous painting of General Washington crossing the Delaware River actually has the first president in what looks like Germany! The German-born painter completed the portrait while staying in Dusseldorf, Germany, and so used the Rhine as his model for the river.

What's more, in the painting, Washington's troops hold aloft a flag with thirteen stars and stripes—a design that wasn't adopted until 1777, a year after the crossing took place! To this day, however, the painting remains the most famous image of America's future president leading his brave but ragged troops to victory.

It was a receptacle of general information. Some years ago, on removing the furniture from the office, I took down the bundle. Immediately underneath the string was a slip bearing this endorsement, in his hand: 'When you can't find it anywhere else, look in this.'"

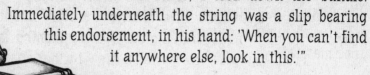

THE MAN TOO TALL TO DUEL

Many of America's presidents have accepted challenges to duels, but none more so than Andrew Jackson, who was involved in more than 100 duels during his lifetime. But it was Abraham Lincoln who, in 1842, found the best way to accept a duel—and knowingly avoid it at the same time!

Lincoln was challenged to a duel by a man named James Shields, who was upset by a letter that Mary Todd, the future president's fiancée, wrote about him to a local newspaper. Accepting the challenge to defend his fiancée's honor, Lincoln was allowed to choose the type of weapon to be used.

He selected broadswords, an especially long type of sword. It was a wise choice, for at 6 feet, 4 inches tall, with long arms to match, our nation's tallest president was too much to conquer, forcing Shields to withdraw his challenge.

EISENHOWER FALLS IN LOVE

Many of America's future presidents have fallen in love with their first ladies at first glance, but none, perhaps, was more smitten than Dwight David Eisenhower, when he met Mamie Doud at a 1915 dinner dance. Asking her for a date, young Dwight was told to "call in a month." Mamie had sorely underestimated the future president's determination, however! Eisenhower called her on the telephone every fifteen minutes throughout the next day until Mamie finally agreed to go out with him. Three months later, the two lovebirds were engaged to be married.

TRICKY DICK
BLUFFS HIS HAND

As a teenager, Richard Nixon learned to play poker while working at a carnival. During his years in the navy, "Tricky Dick" became known as a poker player who could always fool his opponents and who rarely lost. "I once saw him bluff a lieutenant commander out of fifteen hundred dollars with a pair of deuces," said a friend from the time.

Did You Know

... TEDDY ROOSEVELT'S HORSE-RIDING CALVARY DIDN'T RIDE HORSES AT ALL?

"Rough Riders" is the name popularly applied to the 1st Regiment of U.S. Calvary Volunteers in the Spanish-American War. According to newspaper reports at the time (which some people claim were written by Roosevelt himself), Teddy Roosevelt led the Rough Riders on several heroic death-defying calvary raids during the war. Supposedly, he even led America's soldiers on a victorious charge to capture San Juan Hill, located in Cuba. In fact, the future president *did* organize the group but it was commanded by Leonard Wood, a man with far more military experience. What's more, the group's horses had to be left behind in Florida when the calvary left to fight in Cuba, so the "Rough Riders" fought mainly on foot!

MODEL PRESIDENTS

Many of our presidents were considered "model Americans" before running for office, but two of our country's future chief executives actually worked as models on their way to the White House: Gerald Ford and Ronald Reagan. Ford, while studying to become a lawyer, appeared as a fashion model in *Look* magazine and went on to help create the Conover Modeling Agency. Reagan, who was chosen as the man with "the most nearly perfect male figure" by the Fine Arts Department at the University of Southern California, modeled for statues sculpted by the students there.

JIMMY CARTER SEES A UFO!

Alone among America's presidents, Jimmy Carter has reported seeing a UFO (unidentified flying object). The incident occurred on January 6, 1969, while he was waiting for a Lions Club meeting to begin in Leary, Georgia. Forty-year-old Carter, along with ten other eyewitnesses at the scene, decribed the UFO as "bluish at first—then reddish—but not solid. . . . It appeared as bright as the moon."

RONALD REAGAN, LAS VEGAS HEADLINER

In 1954, long before he became president, movie actor Ronald Reagan agreed to star in a stage show at the Ramona Room of the Hotel Last Frontier, in Las Vegas. He introduced other performers, told jokes, and did comedy skits with the "Honey Brothers." The show was a huge success, and Reagan received offers to continue in live theater. Instead, he returned to Hollywood, and launched a career in television.

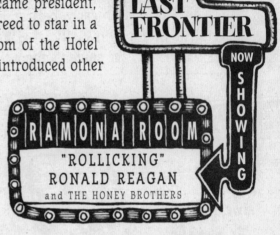

HOTEL LAST FRONTIER

NOW SHOWING

RAMONA ROOM

"ROLLICKING"
RONALD REAGAN
and THE HONEY BROTHERS

PRESIDENTS WHO NEVER WENT TO COLLEGE

Not every president went to such Ivy League schools as Yale University (William Taft and George Bush) or Stanford University (Herbert Hoover). In fact, the following presidents never even went to college:

George Washington
Andrew Jackson
Martin Van Buren
Zachary Taylor
Millard Fillmore

Abraham Lincoln
Andrew Johnson
Grover Cleveland
Harry S Truman

(William Henry Harrison and William McKinley
attended college, but never graduated.)

The road to office is different for every president. Some candidates campaign long and hard for enough votes to beat their opponents; others win their elections easily. Some candidates campaign for the presidency many times, and then there are those who never wanted to become president at all.

THE PRESIDENT WHO DIDN'T EVEN VOTE FOR HIMSELF!

Believe it or not, President Zachary Taylor didn't even vote in his own election! Why? Because he was a professional soldier, Taylor was always moving from place to place. Thus, he never established the official "place of residence" the government requires of American citizens before they can cast a vote. In fact, President Taylor didn't vote in an election until he was retired, at the age of sixty-two!

THE PRESIDENT WHO FACED HIS ASSASSINS

Many who have campaigned for president have also been faced with the threat of assassins at public gatherings on the road to election day. One future president, however, decided to face his would-be assassins as squarely as any other opponent: Andrew Johnson, a rough-hewn frontiersman who didn't frighten easily, received death threats during his campaign for a second term as Tennessee's governor.

During a public speech, he turned to his audience, laid a pistol in front of him, and said: "Fellow citizens, I have been informed that part of the business to be transacted on the present occasion is the assassination of the individual who now has the honor of addressing you. I beg respectfully to propose that this be the first business in order.

Therefore if any man has come here tonight for the purpose indicated, I do not say to him let him speak, but let him shoot."

No one was willing to face the challenge, and Johnson went on to give his campaign speech . . . and win the election.

AND THE PRESIDENT IS . . . OOPS!

Many of our country's elections have been so close that some candidates were forced to go to bed while votes were being counted, uncertain whether they had won or lost. On two occasions, however, newspapers decided they would announce who was president anyway . . . and guessed wrong!

The first occurred during the 1876 campaign, when Republican Rutherford B. Hayes ran against Democrat Samuel Tilden. The *New York Tribune*, eager to print election results in the early morning edition of the paper, announced that Tilden had won the presidency. It took some time for the final votes to be counted, and even three days later Hayes said: "I think we are defeated. Democrats have carried the country and elected Tilden." As it turned out, however, it was Hayes who won, and went on to serve as our nation's 19th president.

The second time this mistake occurred was during the 1948 reelection campaign of Harry S Truman, when political experts predicted he would lose the election to Thomas E. Dewey. With the final votes still being counted, the *Chicago Tribune* decided to print the headline "Dewey Defeats Truman." President Truman won the election and proudly held the newspaper's mistake up for all the world to see.

Did You Know

... ONE TOWN'S NAME CHANGED WITH THE PRESIDENT?

Everybody expects *some* change when a new president is elected, but to citizens of one American town, election results actually changed where they lived! Residents of Adams, New Hampshire (which was first named in 1800 to celebrate the election of John Adams to the presidency) were no doubt pleased to see John Adams's son John Quincy Adams elected president in 1824. But when Adams lost the 1828 election to Andrew Jackson, the town decided to change with the times—renaming itself Jackson, New Hampshire on the spot!

THE PRESIDENT WHO WON NO VOTES

Not all candidates are somebody's favorite choice . . . at first. At the 1880 Republican Convention, where delegates from each of the states voted their choice for the Republican presidential candidate, James A. Garfield received no votes on the first ballot (a ballot is a round of voting). Eventually, though, as the delegates voted again, Garfield went on to win the nomination—and the presidency!

THE SPEECH SO LONG IT SAVED A LIFE

Since the days of George Washington, many American leaders have believed that short speeches are the most effective way to campaign for office, but Theodore Roosevelt once wrote a speech so long it actually saved his life!

In 1912, when the ex-president was campaigning for a third term as the candidate of the independent Bull Moose Party, he appeared at a rally in Milwaukee with a fifty-page speech folded double in his pocket. As fate would have it, an assassin fired a shot directly at Roosevelt, and the bullet passed through the president's coat, vest, eyeglass case, and the hundred pages before entering his chest. Had the speech not slowed and altered the bullet's course, Mr. Roosevelt would have been shot through the heart, and certainly killed.

As it was, the sturdy old cowboy president realized his wounds were not serious and declared: "I am going to make that speech if I die doing it." Roosevelt took the speech out of his pocket and showed the bullet-holed pages to the astonished crowd, then stood and delivered his remarks in their entirety.

THE ONE-DOLLAR HAT TOSS

Even though it was Theodore Roosevelt who popularized the expression "my hat is in the ring" when running for public office, it was Lyndon Johnson who literally tossed his hat on the way to the White House. As a campaigning congressman, Johnson became known for throwing his trademark Stetson out into

Did You Know

. . . WHERE THE TERM "OKAY" COMES FROM?

The familiar expression "O.K." (or "okay") actually comes from the 1840 reelection campaign of President Van Buren! How? Martin Van Buren had grown up in Kinderhook, New York—which was sometimes called "Old Kinderhook." To support Van Buren's campaign, Old Kinderhook Clubs (also called "O.K." clubs) were formed. Although President Van Buren lost the election to William Henry Harrison, "O.K." went on to become a popular saying—meaning "all right," because as far as his supporters were concerned, Martin Van Buren was "all right" with them!

the crowd at political rallies. But Johnson's hat toss wasn't a souvenir to his followers: The money-wise president-to-be always paid a small boy $1 to retrieve the $25 hat for him.

THE LONGEST NOMINATING SPEECH

Which president once gave such a long-winded nominating speech (which officially proposes a political party's candidate for president) that he was "booed" off the stage? Bill Clinton, who was the governor of Arkansas at the time, gave a nominating speech for Michael Dukakis at the 1988 Democratic Convention. It was such a failure that he thought his political career might be over—but Clinton went on to become president himself in the very next election!

Have you ever wondered what you would do if *you were elected president?* What would you change? Would you make school lunch longer? Make the air cleaner? The streets safer? How would you make life better for everybody? The possibilities may seem endless. . . .

Here's a "presidential" mini-project to try on your own, with help from your family and friends, or as a class project. Write or draw your best suggestions to help the president change America, then mail your ideas to:

WHAT WOULD YOU DO AS PRESIDENT?

THE WHITE HOUSE

Executive Office of the President
1600 Pennsylvania Avenue N.W.
Washington, D.C. 20500

Not only will you be helping make America a better place to live . . . with a little help from your president, you could one day see some of your ideas become reality!

Taking the Oath

"I do solemnly swear (or affirm) that I will faithfully execute the office of the president of the United States, and will to the best of my ability, preserve, protect and defend the constitution of the United States."
—The Presidential Oath of Office, Article II, Section I of the U.S. Constitution

This oath was first recited by George Washington, and has been repeated by each president at his own inauguration. Becoming a president, however, has not always been so straightforward. History has produced some amazing stories about presidents taking the oath of office.

AMERICA'S *FIRST* FIRST PRESIDENT

Everybody knows who America's first president was—or do they? In 1781, while George Washington was still fighting the last battles of the Revolution, the thirteen American colonies joined together under the Articles of Confederation and decided the new country needed a leader. The Continental Congress thus elected Maryland representative John Hanson as "President of the United States in Congress Assembled," before America had actually won its independence from England. General Washington himself wrote a letter to President Hanson, congratulating him on his "appointment to fill the most important seat in the United States." President Hanson served the nation honorably for one year before ill health forced him to resign.

Once America was recognized as its own nation, Washington became the nation's first "real" president. However, not all Americans have forgotten this original president: Every year, in Maryland, at least, April 14th is known as John Hanson Day.

THE SHORTEST INAUGURAL ADDRESS

President Washington was an awkward public speaker who preferred to be silent whenever possible. Thus his second inauguration's acceptance speech was the shortest by any president—only 133 words! Whenever Washington spoke, however, people listened with great respect and admiration, for our nation's first president was known as a man who spoke from the heart.

THE PRESIDENT WHO WASN'T REALLY PRESIDENT

In 1841, when President William Henry Harrison became the first president to die in office, there was nothing written in the Constitution that said the vice-president should then become president himself. It said, instead, that the "powers and duties" of the president "shall devolve on the vice-president," which means that the vice-president has the duties of president, but not the title. Vice-president John Tyler, however, decided to call himself president anyway, and every following vice-president who replaced a president followed his example.

It wasn't until 1967, after President Kennedy was assassinated, that Congress passed the 25th Amendment to the Constitution, which formally allows the vice-president to replace the president in duty and name in case of disability, death, resignation, or removal from office.

PRESIDENT FOR A DAY

Although William Henry Harrison served the shortest *official* presidential term, a man named David Atchison was president for a single day! How? In March 1849, Zachary Taylor was to be sworn in as president . . . but because the inauguration was to take place on a Monday and the Constitution designated President Polk's term had ended at noon the day before, neither man was president for that single day. The vice-president had already resigned from the senate, so fellow senators elected Missouri Senator David Rice Atchison to fill his place! Today, on his monument are carved the words: "David Rice Atchison, 1807–1886—President of the U.S. one day."

A DRUNKEN OATH

Can it be that a future American president was drunk when he took his first oath of office? Yes . . . but there's a reason: Andrew Johnson, while being sworn in as vice-president in 1865, was required to drink large amounts of alcohol to ease the pain of typhoid fever. It was the best treatment available in those days!

TAKE A BATH . . . AND BECOME PRESIDENT!

In 1901, after President McKinley was killed by an assassin's bullet, Vice-President Theodore Roosevelt was quickly sworn into office at a small ceremony witnessed by just a few newspaper reporters. One of

the reporters typed up his report of the inauguration as quickly as possible—perhaps too quickly, it seems, accidentally using the letter "b" instead of "o" in the word "oath." When printed the next morning, newspaper subscribers were told that: "For sheer democratic dignity, nothing could exceed the moment when, surrounded by the Cabinet and a few distinguished citizens, Mr. Roosevelt took his simple bath, as president of the United States." Americans everywhere were surprised to hear of their new president's first act in office, and it wasn't until the next day's paper that the mistake could be explained and corrected.

Presidential Days

From the moment he takes the Presidential Oath through the remainder of his term, a president's days are filled with important meetings, formal ceremonies, and elegant celebrations. Here are stories from inside those White House walls.

PRESIDENT JACKSON SURVIVES 1 IN 125,000 ODDS

In addition to his many other firsts, Andrew Jackson was the first president to face an assassination attempt. The incident occurred on January 30, 1835, when Jackson was attending the funeral of a congressman from South Carolina. An Englishman named Richard Lawrence approached the president and fired two pistols at close range. Remarkably, however, both pistols misfired, although each had been loaded properly. A gun expert estimated this might occur once in 125,000 firings! The president was unharmed, and the Englishman, who claimed to be an heir to the British throne, was apprehended, tried, and committed to a mental institution.

ABRAHAM LINCOLN'S "BAD DREAM"

Abraham Lincoln, who was president during the Civil War, received many letters from people threatening to kill him. He began having bad dreams at night, and once dreamt he was walking through the White House and heard many people weeping and sobbing. When he entered the East Room he saw a coffin there. Turning to a soldier he asked: "Who is dead in the White House?" "The president," answered the soldier. "He was killed by an assassin!"

President Lincoln had this dream the night before he went to Ford's Theater to see a play called "Our American Cousin"—where he was assassinated by John Wilkes Booth!

THE PRESIDENT LEARNS GOLF

Ulysses S. Grant, a vigorous man who served two terms as president after leading the Union states to victory in the Civil War, agreed to join a friend at a golf course to witness the new and popular game in action. A golfer stepped up to the ball and began to swing, but dirt and grass flew everywhere as he missed the ball over and over again. The president turned to his friend and said: "That does look like very good exercise, but what is the little white ball for?"

PRESIDENT GARFIELD'S SPECIAL TALENT

James A. Garfield had the rare ability to write equally well with either his left or right hand. Garfield was also able to read and write in ancient Greek and Latin. To amuse his guests, he would write in Greek with one hand while—at the same time—writing in Latin with the other.

PRESIDENT ARTHUR'S BRAVEST BATTLE

Chester A. Arthur was known as a man of culture and ability, a caring politician who could not be corrupted by the business of politics. When he was offered the vice-presidency in 1880, Arthur accepted gratefully, exclaiming: "The office of vice-president is the greatest honor that I ever dreamed of attaining."

Six months later, however, an assassin's bullet killed President Garfield. Arthur, who had never been elected to any public office on his own, found himself unknown and untrusted throughout the nation. He fought hard to show the country that he could be trusted, and soon became a popular leader known for his fairness.

President Arthur's bravest battle, however, was kept secret from the American people for his entire life. During Arthur's years in office the president was dying of Bright's disease, an inflammation of the kidneys. He kept his condition hidden to protect the country from fear of two consecutive presidents dying while in office. Arthur kept up his busy presidential schedule, even though he knew this activity weak-

Did You Know

... WHICH PRESIDENT SHOULD'VE BEEN A PRIEST?

William McKinley was considered a popular and successful president who skillfully led the nation during the Spanish-American War.

In 1900 he easily won reelection to a second term of office, but shortly thereafter, while presiding at the opening of the Pan-American Exposition, McKinley was shot and killed by an assassin named Leon Czolgosz.

As it turns out, he might have fared better had he been a priest. Why? A short while before, Czolgosz, standing in a small Chicago tailor's shop, announced that after thinking about the state of the world he had decided to kill a priest. "Why kill a priest?" he was asked. "There are so many priests." Czolgosz thought about this, and agreed that it would have more impact if he killed a president.

ened his chances of fighting the disease. In the end, he survived his four years in office and lived another year and a half, finally succumbing to the disease in 1886.

THE PRESIDENT WHO KEPT A SECRET IN HIS MOUTH

Every president must be careful about what "secrets" are told to the general public, but did you know that one president died with one of his biggest secrets still hidden—inside his mouth?!

During his second term, Grover Cleveland's doctors discovered a cancer inside his mouth and determined that part of his jaw would have to be removed to save the president's life. President Cleveland was concerned about what the public might think of this operation and so decided to have the surgery performed secretly at night, aboard a yacht anchored on the East River in New York City. The operation was a success, and the cancerous jawbone was replaced with a matching piece of rubber, all of it hidden inside the president's mouth.

When word leaked out about the operation to the newspapers, the president and his close friends denied the story. It wasn't until 1917, almost twenty-five years later and nine years after Grover Cleveland's death, that the truth was finally published in an article in the *Saturday Evening Post.*

THE TEDDY BEAR IS BORN

In 1902, Teddy Roosevelt went on a bear hunting trip in Mississippi, but only found one bear. It was a small, abandoned bear cub, an easy target for the expert marksman. But Teddy could not shoot it; he just plain refused. The story of Teddy's compassion got around and the *Washington Post* newspaper ran a cartoon showing Teddy and his tiny bear cub. A few days later, a toy store owner in Brooklyn, New York placed the cartoon in his window next to a cuddly stuffed bear, which he called "Teddy's Bear." Thus the teddy bear was born.

MR. RUCEVELT CHANGIZ
THE INGLISH LANGGWIDG

Presidents are responsible for many changes that affect our daily lives, but Theodore Roosevelt once tried to change the English language itself!

On August 27, 1906, while Congress was out of session, President Roosevelt ordered the public printer to "simplify" the spelling of 300 words in all government publications—changing "kissed" to "kist," "blushed" to "blusht," and "through" to "thru," among others. The changes were not popular with the public, and the editor of the *Louisville Courier-Journal* wrote an angry editorial in the newspaper: "Nuthing escapes Mr. Rucevelt. No subject is tu hi fr him to takl, nor tu lo for him tu notis. He makes tretis without the consent of the Senit. He inforces such laws as meet his approval, and fales to se those that du not soot him. He now assales the English langgwidg, constitutes himself a sort of French Academy, and will reform the spelling in a way tu soot himself."

After Congress returned to session, Roosevelt's edict was quickly overturned. A resolution enforced ordering the Government Printing Office to return to the traditional spellings.

THE FIRST FLOCK

In 1917, President Woodrow Wilson decided sheep could trim the White House lawn instead of hiring men who could be better used to help the national war effort during World War I. The flock of sheep grazed contentedly around the White House grounds, eating not just the grass but expensive shrubs and flowers.

Many people began to complain that the White House was being destroyed, but Mrs. Wilson insisted that the sheep were doing their part to help the country . . . even producing ninety-eight pounds of wool, sold to raise money for the Red Cross. The sheep became very popular with children around the country, especially a tobacco-chewing ram named Old Ike, who liked to eat cigar stubs.

THE PRESIDENT
WHO CURED BALDNESS

Throughout history men have sought a solution to cure their baldness, but one U.S. president took the matter into his own hands. Calvin Coolidge, who was balding himself, never liked the portrait of John Adams visible from his seat in the state dining room, in particular because of Adams' prominent bald head. Rather than move the painting to a new location, Coolidge asked the White House's chief usher, Ike Hoover, to "put some hair on Adams' head."

The usher obeyed, and added some turpentine to that portion of the painting, removing the shine and giving America's first bald president the impression of having a little hair. President Coolidge was very satisfied with the alteration.

Did You Know

. . . WHICH PRESIDENT WANTED TO BE A PRO ATHLETE?

George Bush studied economics while in college at Yale, but his heart was really set on a future in sports. Bush especially enjoyed playing soccer and baseball, and played first base on a team that won the Eastern Regional Championship in 1947 and 1948. In the newspapers, the young ballplayer was called "impressive" and "a classy first baseman."

Bush claimed his talent came from his mother, whom he described as "a first-rate athlete. She wasn't big, but she was a match for anyone in tennis, golf, basketball, or baseball." George dreamed of playing professional sports, but the opportunity never came. When he became president, he installed a horseshoe throwing pit on the White House grounds, and took to jogging and fishing instead.

THE PRESIDENT'S BEST FRIEND WAS AN INFORMER!

For safety's sake, President Franklin Delano Roosevelt's travel schedule was kept "top secret" during the busy years of World War II. Reporters found themselves searching for someone close to the president who could provide them with clues to his comings and goings. Thus it was that the president's favorite and constant companion, Fala, a Scottish terrier, was given the nickname "the informer." Reporters had figured out that Secret Service agents took Fala for a brief walk at every train stop. They used that as their cue that the president was traveling aboard the train.

THE DAY THE PRESIDENT WAS TORPEDOED

Every war produces tragedies where soldiers are accidentally killed by their own country in what is called "friendly fire." But on November 14, 1943, the unlucky near-victim of just one such mishap was none other than Franklin Delano Roosevelt, president of the United States!

The president and his staff were crossing the Atlantic aboard the U.S. battleship *Iowa* to attend a secret conference in Cairo when the Navy destroyer *William D. Porter* accidentally fired a live torpedo during a simulated defense exercise in the area. The torpedo headed straight for the president's ship, which made a high-speed turn in hopes of avoiding the line of fire. Fortunately, the torpedo exploded in the churning waves created by the *Iowa*, and disaster was avoided.

A PRESIDENTIAL REMINDER
. . . BRUSH TWICE A DAY

America's presidents receive gifts from friends and admirers around the world, and some presidents enjoy returning the favor, giving away mementos whenever possible. Lyndon Johnson spent three times as much on gifts during his first year in office than Kennedy before him. The gift he liked to give the most was . . . the electric toothbrush!

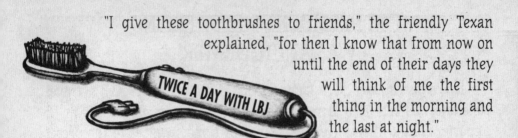

"I give these toothbrushes to friends," the friendly Texan explained, "for then I know that from now on until the end of their days they will think of me the first thing in the morning and the last at night."

THE TEMPORARY PRESIDENT

George Bush came into the presidency with more than just eight years of vice-presidential experience—he had actually served as president for seven hours and fifty-four minutes during his years in the Reagan Administration! On July 13, 1985, President Reagan underwent surgery to remove a cancer from his intestine. Just before he was put to sleep for the operation, Reagan transferred the powers of the presidency to Vice-President Bush. After the surgery was completed and Reagan regained consciousness, all presidential authority was returned to him. Bush is the only person who has gone from being vice-president to president and back to vice-president again—before being elected to the presidency himself!

Did You Know

... THE EMANCIPATION PROCLAMATION FREED NO SLAVES?

It is a common misconception that President Lincoln's "Emancipation Proclamation," issued in 1862, freed America's slaves. In fact, the document had no legal force, freed no slaves whatsoever, and was promptly ignored by all those affected by the declaration. Why? The Emancipation Proclamation declared slaves free in Confederate States only, and since the Confederacy was at war with the United States at the time, it was considered little more than a political statement meant to build support for Lincoln's war effort.

PINCHING THOSE PRESIDENTIAL PENNIES

Because being president of the United States is considered a form of public service, the job has never paid as well as many other jobs with far less responsibility. Here is a list of presidential salaries throughout America's history.

GEORGE WASHINGTON thru ANDREW JOHNSON — $25,000 per year

ULYSSES S. GRANT thru THEODORE ROOSEVELT — $50,000 per year
(President Grant received $25,000 per year for his 1st term, and $50,000 per year during his 2nd term)

WILLIAM HOWARD TAFT thru FRANKLIN D. ROOSEVELT — $75,000 per year
(plus a $25,000 travel allowance)

HARRY S TRUMAN thru LYNDON B. JOHNSON — $100,000 per year
(plus $40,000 for travel and entertainment, and a $50,000 per year expense account)

RICHARD M. NIXON thru BILL CLINTON — $200,000 per year
(plus $100,000 for travel, $12,000 for entertainment, and a $50,000 per year expense account)

First Ladies

Presidents' wives are not elected or paid and have no constitutional power in government, but history has shown they're often as important to the success of a presidency as the president himself.

The term "first lady" seems to have originated at the inauguration of Rutherford Hayes, in 1877, when a reporter respectfully referred to his wife as "Lucy, the First Lady." By 1911, a play about President Madison's wife Dolley called "The First Lady in the Land" was a hit across the nation. From that point on, all presidential wives were called "first ladies."

FIRST LADY TO TWO PRESIDENTS?

Dolley Madison, wife to President James Madison, is considered one of the most popular and successful first ladies in America's history, especially in her duties as the nation's White House hostess. But there was good reason: unlike any other first lady, she had served as the White House hostess before her husband ever held the presidency. Why? Since Thomas Jefferson's own wife died before he became president, Dolley, whose husband served as secretary of state at the time, functioned as hostess at all White House functions.

THE SHADOW IN THE WHITE HOUSE

Not all first ladies have enjoyed their role as White House hostess. Franklin Pierce's wife Jane never once appeared in public for the entire first two years of his term in office, not even at the fourteenth president's inaugural ball. Newspaper editors began to call the first lady "the shadow in the White House." During this time, Mrs. Pierce remained in her bedroom, distraught over the death of her eleven-year-old son Bennie, who had been killed in a railway accident two months before the president's swearing-in. When she finally appeared in public, at an 1855 New Year's reception, the first lady was dressed in mourning clothes, which she wore for the rest of her life.

THE FIRST LADY
WHOSE DRINKS PACKED A PUNCH

When Rutherford B. Hayes became president in 1877, he and his wife Lucy decided to set an example for the nation by banning all wine and liquor from the White House. It was not a popular decision among guests and visitors, however. The first lady soon acquired the nickname "Lemonade Lucy," since lemonade was the strongest drink she made available at White House parties.

Eventually, guests thought they'd found a way to sneak a drink for themselves, convincing the serving stewards to add smuggled rum to the lemonade and fruit punch usually served. The president and his wife, however, had the last laugh, for they knew what the guests were up to, and purposely had the drinks flavored to taste like rum . . . without a single drop of added alcohol!

VOTE FOR THE FIRST LADY
. . . AND THE PRESIDENT, TOO!

James Buchanan and Grover Cleveland were the only two bachelors ever elected president, but Grover Cleveland changed all that by becoming the only president ever to marry while in the White House. His bride, Frances Folsom, twenty-one years old, was the youngest first lady this country has ever known—and also one of the most popular and beautiful.

Women throughout America eagerly looked for pictures of the first lady so they could copy her latest hairstyle. When President Cleveland ran for a second term he decided to put *her* picture on campaign posters along with himself and the vice-president—something that's never happened before or since!

THE "PETTICOAT GOVERNMENT"

Will America ever elect a woman president? They may have already had one, without even knowing it!

President Woodrow Wilson, who led the nation through the first World War, suffered a paralyzing stroke on September 26, 1919, and was confined to bed for a period of many months. First Lady Edith Wilson suspended all her hostess duties at the White House and became her husband's caretaker, presenting presidential matters to him daily and relaying his wishes to the outside world. Because of this, Wilson's presidential administration was sometimes referred to as the "petticoat government" (a petticoat was a woman's underskirt commonly worn in those days). If the same thing were to happen today, people would say she "wears the pants in the family!"

FIRST LADY, FIRST GIRL SCOUT

President Hoover's wife Lou was, like her husband, a very educated person. Together they published a 640-page book about metallurgy, the science of extracting and refining metals from ore. So for this first lady, the traditional role of White House hostess and homemaker was not enough to keep her busy.

Lou Hoover soon became one of the first "activist" first ladies, working for the League of Women Voters, the General Federation of Women's Clubs, and even becoming president of the Girl Scouts of America!

ROVER TRAVELS THE WORLD

Like her uncle, Theodore Roosevelt, Eleanor Roosevelt had many interests and boundless energy. Often called "First Lady of the World," she set a new standard during her thirteen years in the White House and became a role model to generations of modern women.

Eleanor became a spokesperson for women's rights, helped promote work programs for the unemployed, spoke out against racial discrimination, and wrote her own daily newspaper column. She received more than 250,000 letters from the public each year, answering a good portion of them herself.

The first woman to hold a news conference in the White House, Eleanor Roosevelt reported to the public about her many activities around the world. The first lady traveled so often that she had a special code name, "Rover," given to her by the Secret Service men who protected her.

LADY BIRD MAKES AMERICA BEAUTIFUL

Claudia Taylor was given the nickname "Lady Bird" by a nursemaid when she was just a baby. She used the name for the rest of her life to convey her love of nature. When she married Lyndon Johnson and went on to become first lady, Lady Bird Johnson developed a national "beautification" program to improve America's cities and rural highways.

While in the White House, Lady Bird traveled more than 200,000 miles to promote a more beautiful America, encouraging people to feel proud about their neighborhoods. She helped open new parks and gardens in cities everywhere, and played a key role in creating the Highway Beautification Act of 1965, which limited how many advertising billboards could be placed on highways. Lady Bird was one first lady who put beauty first in the nation.

Family Life

It's easy to forget that even though the White House is the official office for the business of the United States government, it's also been called "home" by forty-two presidential families. The nearly two hundred children and grandchildren who have lived and played there have discovered just how interesting family life in the executive mansion can be.

HELP WANTED: SEE THE PRESIDENT FOR DETAILS

Presidents today have million-dollar household budgets, with government officials who hire the cooks, cleaners, drivers, and everything else needed to keep the White House running smoothly. But it wasn't always that way. George Washington had to put his own ads in the newspaper to hire servants while he was president!

On December 19, 1789, shortly after they began their first term in office, the First Family ran two ads in the *New York Daily Gazette,*

Did You Know

. . . WASHINGTON'S TEETH WEREN'T MADE OF WOOD?

Everybody has heard that George Washington wore false teeth made of wood . . . but in truth, Washington's dentures were made from much stronger stuff. Our nation's first leader, who had but a single natural tooth left by the time he became president, wore dentures made from cow's teeth, hippopotamus teeth, carved elephant tusks, walrus tusks, and even other human teeth!

seeking a cook "for the Family of the President" and a coachman "well-recommended for his skill in driving and attention to horses."

The ads ran for nearly six weeks, for good help was hard to find. The Washingtons hired twenty-one servants in total, on an average yearly White House budget of only $30,000!

THE WHITE HOUSE'S FIRST LAUNDRY ROOM

John and Abigail Adams were the first First Family to live in the White House, which was still being designed and built during Washington's years as president. They arrived to find the great mansion still unfinished, with wet, slow-drying walls, making the house very cold indeed. Being very practical people, they burned large amounts of firewood every day until the walls were finally dry. In the meantime, Abigail used the unfinished East Room to hang out the wet laundry.

THE PRESIDENTIAL BIRDFEEDER

Many of our country's presidents have had a favorite pet, but there was one president who made sure his special companion received real "presidential" treatment. Thomas Jefferson kept a mockingbird named Dick in the White House study, and let the bird ride on his shoulder whenever possible. President Jefferson even trained Dick to take bits of food that he held between his lips at meals! When Jefferson went upstairs, his faithful companion would hop up after him, step after step, never far from his side.

THE WHITE HOUSE CIRCUS

Theodore Roosevelt had six children and encouraged them to lead active and adventuresome lives. The newspapers often told stories of their activities in the White House, which sometimes seemed more like a circus than America's seat of government.

One of the Roosevelt children's favorite games involved using large serving platters to slide down the White House's main staircase. Teddy's son Quentin once snuck his pony Algonquin upstairs to cheer up his older brother Archie, who was sick with the measles. Roosevelt's teenage daughter Alice was the most rambunctious of all. She loved creating a sensation by smoking in public and betting on horses at the racetracks—not the sort of activities proper women were supposed to engage in at the time, especially a president's daughter!

Newspaper reporters asked President Roosevelt what he was going to do about his daughter's behavior. The president only smiled and said, "I can run the country or control Alice, but not both."

FRESH MILK FOR ALL

First Lady Helen Taft fell ill during part of her husband's years as president, but she knew the three Taft children would be well cared for because President Taft took a special interest in their health himself. He liked milk and insisted that the children drink it fresh every day, so the president kept a cow on the White House lawn to be milked each morning!

Did You Know

... WHICH PRESIDENT LOVED TO SMOKE CIGARS, BUT NEVER SHOWED IT?

William McKinley loved to smoke cigars, but few Americans realized it while he was president. Although McKinley continued to smoke throughout his term in office, he made certain to hide his cigar whenever photographers took pictures of him. "The children of America must not see their president smoking," he said, feeling it would set a bad example for the nation.

WASHINGTON'S TOP DOG

No White House pet was more popular than President Harding's Airedale "Laddie Boy." Like many dogs, Laddie Boy, who owned Washington Dog License Number 1, delivered the president's newspapers to him every morning. In return, Laddie Boy had his own White House valet, and once even had a birthday party with a frosted cake made of layered dog biscuits!

When President Harding died, the Newsboys' Association, in honor of Laddie Boy's dedicated "newspaper service," erected a statue of the dog in the Smithsonian Institution—where it stands, faithful to this day!

THE DARK HOUSE

Many young children are afraid of the dark at night, so it's lucky that President Lyndon Johnson's daughters Lynda and Luci were already teenagers by the time their family moved into the White House. President Johnson was so concerned about not wasting taxpayers' money that he often went through the house at night turning out all the lights! When the newspapers told stories of this, the president was promptly given the nickname "Lightbulb Johnson."

THE CHIEF
. . . POTATO MASHER?

No matter how successful or famous a person becomes, some family traditions never die. Richard Nixon, who spent most of his life campaigning for and working toward the day he became our nation's 37th president, was described by his mother as having some special talents: "He was the best potato masher one could wish for. When I visited Dick or he visited me, [the president] took over the potato mashing. My feeling is that he actually enjoy[ed] it."

Presidential Pets

The White House has been home to almost every type of pet imaginable. From horses to goats, raccoons to roosters, and sheep to alligators, here are a few examples of some famous and not-so-famous presidential pets:

THOMAS JEFFERSON	mockingbird named Dick
WILLIAM HENRY HARRISON	goat
ZACHARY TAYLOR	horse named Whitey
CHESTER A. ARTHUR	pinto pony
BENJAMIN HARRISON	goat named His Whiskers, and a dog
THEODORE ROOSEVELT	one-legged rooster, garter snake, parrot named Eli, pony named Algonquin, bear named Jonathon, and a guinea pig named Father Grandy
WILLIAM HOWARD TAFT	cow named Pauline
WOODROW WILSON	sheep, and a ram named Old Ike
WARREN G. HARDING	airedale named Laddie Boy
CALVIN COOLIDGE	raccoon, goose, wallaby, donkey, thrush, lion cub, two cats, twelve dogs, birds, and a collie named Rob Roy
HERBERT HOOVER	two alligators
FRANKLIN ROOSEVELT	scottie dog named Fala
JOHN KENNEDY	dog named Pushinka, three ponies (one named Marconi), cat, horse, hamster, and a rabbit
LYNDON JOHNSON	two beagles named Him and Her
RICHARD NIXON	cocker spaniel named Checkers
GERALD FORD	golden retriever named Liberty
JIMMY CARTER	dog named Grits, siamese cat named Misty Malarky Ying Yang
GEORGE BUSH	dog named Millie
BILL CLINTON	cat named Socks

It has often been said that the White House belongs to the people of the United States, and in former times any citizen *could*, in fact, walk in and greet members of the First Family. Today there are still ways you can contact the White House, such as writing to the White

Contact the White House!

House (see address on page 67). You can also send messages to the president or anyone else at the White House through electronic mail [usually called "e-mail"] at the White House "web site," accessed through a computer.

The White House web site address: **http://www.whitehouse.gov**

At the web site, you will be welcomed to the White House. There's a lot to explore:

1. **President's Welcome Message**: a message from the president.
2. **Vice-President's Welcome Message**: a message from the vice-president.
3. **Guest Book**: a place to write in your own e-mail address.
4. **Executive Branch**: a map of Washington, D.C. and information on the president and his Cabinet.
5. **First Family**: stories and pictures about the president's inauguration, and more.
6. **Tours**: a place to visit the White House, take the First Lady's "Garden Tour," explore the Old Executive Office Building, and more.
7. **What's New**: recent presidential speeches, connect to the Senate, and explore "what's new" clippings from the past.
8. **Publications**: contains daily press releases, major presidential documents, budget notes, technology notes, and copies of both the Declaration of Independence and the Constitution.
9. **Comments**: how to send a message to the president or vice-president.

America's presidents have taken different roads after their term as chief executive. Some have enjoyed retirement, others have embarked on new careers, while others have remained active in government. Some presidents have found themselves quickly forgotten, while others have been honored and remembered in countless ways.

THE JOYS OF PLANTATION LIVING

Believe it or not, George Washington had to be convinced that it was his duty to the nation to serve in the Continental Congress, and later as America's first leader. The general who had led America's troops to victory in the Revolutionary War wanted nothing more than to retire to his Mount Vernon plantation, where he could pursue the life of an independent farmer.

After the inauguration of his successor, John Adams, Washington did just that, quickly settling into the business of overseeing his much-neglected property. It was on one such horseback tour of his estate that Washington caught cold from a winter storm. By the next day, the cold had worsened and despite his doctors' best efforts, Washington died. He passed away living out his dream as a plantation farmer.

THE "SICKLY" PRESIDENT
WHO LIVED THE LONGEST

President John Adams considered himself "sick" and "near death" throughout much of his life—yet lived longer than any other president! Adams, who helped draft the Declaration of Independence and served as America's second president, complained that his health was "feeble" at age thirty-five. By age thirty-seven he declared himself "an infirm man." But Adams survived to celebrate the fiftieth anniversary of his country's independence!

Not until age ninety did Adams pass away, while seated at his family estate in Braintree, Massachusetts.

A NEW CAREER . . . IN POLITICS AGAIN

John Quincy Adams, President Adams' son, had enjoyed a life in politics since his early boyhood. After being defeated for reelection in 1828 he retired reluctantly, assuming he would have to spend his final years writing books and speaking about events of the past. But it was not to be.

In 1830, a group of his Massachusetts neighbors approached Adams and asked him to run for the House of Representatives. John Quincy Adams jumped at the chance, easily defeating his opponent.

On December 5, 1831, he began what was to become a long and successful second career in politics, earning the nickname "Old Man Eloquent" for his many words of wisdom. John Quincy Adams continued to serve his nation until 1848, when he suffered a stroke while seated in House chambers.

THE MEMOIRS THAT RACED AGAINST TIME

Ulysses S. Grant, the tough, cigar-smoking general who led the Union to victory in the Civil War and served as president for eight years, was eager to be elected for a third term in office. When that failed to happen, he realized that, like many former presidents, he barely had enough money to retire and had no income to leave his family after his death.

After several failed business investments, Grant decided to write his memoirs. As bad luck would have it, just as he began writing he was diagnosed with throat cancer, and so Grant spent his last years racing against time to leave his legacy behind. Upon finishing the two-volume autobiography in July 1885, he wrote to his doctor: "I am not likely to be more ready to go than at this moment." A couple of weeks later Grant was dead, at the age of sixty-three. His memoirs were a tremendous success, leaving his family the financial security Grant so much desired.

THE THIRTY-ONE YEAR RETIREMENT

Herbert Hoover lived longer after retiring from office than any other president except John Adams. Since Hoover left the White House in the midst of the Great Depression, his personal popularity was very low. In the years following, however, Hoover worked hard to regain the public's approval by chairing several relief organizations during and after World War II.

When Hoover died in 1964, he had risen to become one of the most-loved and respected ex-presidents in American history.

THE PRESIDENT WHO CONTINUES TO SERVE

Like many former presidents, Jimmy Carter left the White House convinced he had much more to give the nation; he felt determined to find a way to continue his public service. In the years since his "retirement" began, Carter has written several books, made goodwill tours of foreign countries, and become a trusted representative of honesty and integrity throughout the world.

Ex-president Carter often oversees democratic elections in foreign lands, helping to ensure they are fair and representative of the people's desires. He also has continued to mediate peace agreements throughout the world, as he did between Egypt and Israel during his presidency. Both Jimmy and his wife Rosalyn donate much of their time to the Habitat for Humanity, an organization devoted to providing inexpensive housing to people around the world.

to do

1. monitor elections
2. peace talks
3. build houses
4. memoirs

Legends Left Behind

Around the country, past U.S. presidents have countless places named after them, from busy streets and highways to schools and libraries. A few presidents have left behind more personal mementos to be remembered by.

THE FIRST HORSE

Much has been written about favorite pets and other animal friends of America's First Families, but perhaps the most touching memory of all can be found on a gravestone in the state of Virginia. There, in an inscription written by President John Tyler is this memorial: "Here lies the body of my good horse, 'The General.' For twenty years he bore me around the circuit of my practice, and in all that time he never made a blunder. Would that his master could say the same!"

THE POLK MEMORIAL ESTATE

After his single term as president, James Polk, who was ill and dying, set about preparing his last will and testament. Above all else, he insisted his estate pass to his beloved wife Sarah, and that after her death they be buried side by side. In addition, Polk requested that after both of their deaths his estate not be sold to strangers—even though he had no children or other legal heirs.

As it happened, the president's wishes were granted, though not as he might have imagined: After Polk's death, Sarah lived for another forty-two years, and upon her death she was indeed buried by his side on the Polk estate. But before a "stranger" could buy the estate, the city government bought the home and tore it down to make room for new roads and businesses. The graves of President Polk and his wife were moved to the Tennessee state capitol, where they remain, side by side to this very day.

THE PRESIDENTIAL PILLOW

Every president, upon taking the oath of office, swears to uphold and defend the United States Constitution "to the best of his abilities" while leading the nation, but one president, at least, carried this oath to his final days . . . and beyond! Andrew Johnson, who died on July 31, 1875, had a replica of the Constitution buried along with his remains—as a pillow under his head!

How the Presidents Died

Washington	pneumonia	B. Harrison	pneumonia
J. Adams	debility	McKinley	assassination
Jefferson	diarrhea	T. Roosevelt	inflammatory
Madison	debility		rheumatism
Monroe	debility	Taft	debility
J.Q. Adams	paralysis	Wilson	apoplexy
Jackson	dropsy	Harding	apoplexy
Van Buren	asthma	Coolidge	heart failure
W.H. Harrison	pneumonia	Hoover	gastrointestinal
Tyler	bilious fever		bleeding
Polk	diarrhea	F.D. Roosevelt	cerebral
Taylor	bilious fever		hemmorage
Fillmore	debility	Truman	cardiovascular
Pierce	stomach		collapse
	inflammation	Eisenhower	heart disease
Buchanan	rheumatic gout	Kennedy	assassination
Lincoln	assassination	L.B. Johnson	heart failure
A. Johnson	paralysis	Nixon	stroke
Grant	cancer	Ford	---
Hayes	heart disease	Carter	---
Garfield	assassination	Reagan	---
Arthur	Bright's disease	Bush	---
Cleveland	debility	Clinton	---

NOTE: *debility* is a general word for dying of "old age"

Index

Adams, John, 9-10, 85, 91-92
Adams, John Quincy, 14-15, 65, 92
Arthur, Chester A., 31-32, 72-73
assassins, 63-64, 65-66, 69, 71, 72, 73
Atchison, David Rice, 69-70

birthplaces of presidents, 56
Buchanan, James, 24-25, 81
Bush, George, 51-52, 76, 78

campaigns, presidential, 63-67
Carter, Jimmy, 49-50, 55, 61-62, 93
Cleveland, Grover, 32-33, 73-74, 82
Clinton, Bill, 53-54, 67
Congress, U.S., 6
Coolidge, Calvin, 40-41, 76

Davis, Jefferson, 57-58
death, causes of, 95
Democratic Party, 15
Democratic-Republican Party, 11

Eisenhower, Dwight D., 44-45
Eisenhower, Mamie, 59-60

family life, 84-88
Federalist Party, 9
Fillmore, Millard, 22-23, 57
Ford, Gerald R., 48-49, 61

Garfield, James A., 30-31, 65, 72
government, U.S., branches, 6-7

Grant, Ulysses S., 28-29, 72, 92-93

Hanson, John, 68
Harding, Warren G., 39-40, 87
Harrison, Benjamin, 33-34
Harrison, William Henry, 17-18, 69, 81
Hayes, Rutherford B., 29, 64
Hoover, Herbert, 41-42, 82, 93

inaugural experiences, 68-70

Jackson, Andrew, 15-16, 71
Jefferson, Thomas, 10-11, 54, 85
Johnson, Andrew, 26-28, 57, 63-64, 70
Johnson, Lady Bird, 83
Johnson, Lyndon B., 46-47, 55, 66-67, 77-78, 87

Kennedy, John F., 45-46

Lincoln, Abraham, 25-26, 58-59, 71, 78

McKinley, William, 34-35, 73, 87
Madison, Dolley, 80
Madison, James, 11-12, 80
Monroe, James, 12-13

National Union Party, 27
Nixon, Richard M., 47-48, 60, 88

pets, 77, 85, 87, 88-89

Pierce, Franklin, 23-24, 80-81
Polk, James, 19-20, 54, 94

Reagan, Ronald, 50-51, 61, 62
Republican Party, 26
retirement years, 91-93

Roosevelt, Eleanor, 83
Roosevelt, Franklin D., 42-43, 77
Roosevelt, Theodore, 36-37, 55, 60, 65-66, 70, 74-75, 85-86

salaries, presidential, 79

Taft, Helen, 86
Taft, William Howard, 37, 86
Taylor, Zachary, 21-22, 57-58, 63
Truman, Harry S, 43-44, 64
Tyler, John, 18-19, 94

Van Buren, Martin, 16-17, 66

Washington, George, 8-9, 58, 69, 84-85, 91
White House, 75
    address, 67
    family life in, 84-88
    pets in, 85, 87, 88-89
    web site address, 90
Wilson, Edith, 75, 82
Wilson, Woodrow, 38, 75, 82
wives of presidents, 80-83